# FINANCIAL
# FEMINISM

# FINANCIAL FEMINISM

## A WOMAN'S GUIDE TO
## INVESTING FOR
## A SUSTAINABLE FUTURE

# JESSICA ROBINSON

unbound

First published in 2021

Unbound
Level 1, Devonshire House, One Mayfair Place, London W1J 8AJ
www.unbound.com

The content in this book is the opinion of the author and is for
general informational purposes only. It is not and in no way can
be construed as professional advice. Should you need professional
advice on your personal financial and investment situation, you
should seek the counsel of a qualified investment professional.

Text design by PDQ Digital Media Solutions Ltd

A CIP record for this book is available from the British Library

ISBN 978-1-78352-952-0 (paperback)
ISBN 978-1-78352-953-7 (ebook)

Printed and bound in Great Britain by Clays Ltd, Elcograf S.p.A.

1 3 5 7 9 8 6 4 2

*To my beautiful and compassionate children, Thalia, Xiaoli and Zander, who know their only job in life is to make the world a better place than when they arrived...*

# CONTENTS

## Part II

## Part III

# PREFACE

Do you ever wake up with an overwhelming feeling that you are not doing enough? Do you ever fear that you are part of the actual problem? You are not alone.

We are watching the Amazon rainforest burn, millions of people struggle to survive because they are living in absolute poverty, children unable to get basic healthcare or go to school. Yet here I find myself, living a life of privilege, consuming what I want, taking more than I give. It's not sitting comfortably, not comfortably at all.

Yes, I have made some changes.

As a consumer, I do my best to buy local and I'm about 80 per cent vegan. My household is as plastic free as possible, and by paying for recycling services I alleviate some of my daily guilt over the amount of trash we generate. As a mother, I preach the values of sustainability, of mindful consumption, of the importance of human rights for all people. My children could probably recite the United Nations 17 Sustainable Development Goals (please don't let me down, kids!).

I work as a strategic advisor to governments, think-tanks, institutional investors and companies, on all matters relating to sustainable finance and responsible investing. And I have done for many years. Yet, despite dedicating my career to this cause, I still feel that I'm falling miserably short. I'm sure there is a lot more that I can do. I know that I am not the only person, and certainly not the only woman, who feels this way.

So I guess that's what this book is. An ardent, urgent attempt to do more, to encourage us all to think about things differently, in an aspect of our lives that we – especially women – so easily overlook: MONEY. I'm taking what I know about professionally and sharing what I'm learning about personally, in the hope that it provides you with some guidance or support in your own journey. Come with me.

## LET'S GET PERSONAL

I've been working in the field of sustainable finance and responsible investing for well over a decade, which is actually quite a long time given the nascency of this area. How did I end up there? Well, I'd say I always cared deeply about social justice and equality. I had the good fortune of growing up in a family who held strong values around the importance of helping people in need, of thinking about the greater good. Intellectually that has always made sense to me and, as a student of economics and politics, I've always been intensely interested in figuring out social systems that delivered for everyone, not just the small elite.

I entered the workforce at a time where fast fashion was becoming a thing (when it became not only affordable but also acceptable to buy an outfit for the weekend and then discard it) and people around me were getting crazily rich, crazily quick during the dot-com era. It was a strange time and I could already sense some internal conflict going on inside my twenty-something head.

However, it wasn't until I became a mother that I really started to see beyond the here and now. It was no longer about me, but about my children's future. This also coincided with a move to Beijing, where environmental problems were just becoming visible to the masses. Air pollution was a real issue: we'd wake up to unnaturally yellow skies and walking outside would leave our clothes smelling horribly sulphuric. I spent a small fortune on home air purifiers, scared of the damage being done to the lungs of my young babies.

And that's when it hit me – here we were, consuming at breakneck speed, while we were quite literally poisoning ourselves because of it. What really scared me was that it seemed that very few people could see this, or perhaps they didn't want to. That may seem ridiculous given what we know now but, at the time, no one (or certainly no one in my world) seemed willing to acknowledge the problem and that frustrated the hell out of me. What happened then was a massive internal awakening. I wanted to change the world and I wanted to change it overnight.

Unfortunately, that didn't quite happen, but I went back to school to study environmental economics and started on a new journey professionally. I began to see how our financial markets were leading us down the wrong path. It became apparent that we were using money purely as an instrument for short-term gain. As I dug deeper into the whole notion of investing, I could see we were getting it all wrong.

Let me explain.

When you think about how investing is defined – allocating money (or capital) to some kind of endeavour (whether it's a company, a project or something else) with the hope of some future benefit – you can see how this has been manipulated. We have been told that the only future benefit worth chasing is… wait for it… more money.

But what if we, as compassionate and caring humans, want to aim for something bigger? And what if 'future benefit' actually means something quite beyond bigger financial returns, beyond more money? What if 'future benefit' reflected our desire to move towards a world that is cleaner? Fairer? More equitable? Dare I say it, happier?

That's how I got involved in sustainable finance and responsible investment. I was looking for ways to marry what I had learned in my earlier career – as a management consultant in the financial services industry – with my increasingly burning passion for all things related to sustainability. It became apparent to me that we needed to start asking questions about what money is, about what capital is – deep and meaningful philosophical questions about what it represents to us as human beings in an increasingly crowded world where resources are no longer abundant, where our systems are clearly failing the majority of people.

## THE WAY I SEE IT

I know I'm not alone in wrestling with these deep questions, because in the last few years, I have seen such a rapid uptick in interest in the power of money and what it can do for the greater good. I mean, even the *Financial Times* now has a regular newsletter entitled 'Moral Money'![1] That's got to tell you something.

To me, money should be a force for good. That means we should be deploying capital to invest in activities that bring real, constructive benefits to the majority of people, people across the world. At the same time, we should not be investing in companies or sectors that bring harm to people. Yes, for sure, there are a whole heap of issues and challenges related to how we measure benefits or identify what we mean by harm. But at no point do those issues and challenges mean we shouldn't be trying.

I believe the fact we have got it so wrong thus far means we are facing a systemic failure, and, in turn, that means we can no longer bury our heads in the sand. Our systems need to change to address this failure. The turbulent events of 2020 have taught us that we need new ways of thinking about things. Even more importantly, we need new ways of doing things.

Sustainable investing presents a lens through which we can look at our world and the personal and societal goals we set. When we choose to invest, when we select an equity or a fund, we are making a choice of one thing over another. We are exposing our preference in the same way we do as consumers, when we choose to buy one product over another. We are not just talking about the role of money. We are talking about the role of companies and sectors, and actively making decisions on the ones we want to be winners.

This is a big deal because if we accept that we have an ability to make informed investment decisions – and we are seeking something beyond just making more money – it inevitably forces us to question the purpose of companies and the role that they play in society. It's also really empowering to see the different levers of change we have at our disposal.

## WHY AM I FOCUSING ON WOMEN?

I, for one, am tired of the way things are and being told we cannot have an impact. The rules of the game can change but it's highly likely that it is we women who will have to change them ourselves.

I genuinely believe that sustainable investing presents an opportunity for women like you and me to start influencing other aspects of our collective lives. We don't have to be pawns in the financial world, where someone else makes decisions on our behalf. We can educate and empower ourselves to demand better from the financial industry.

The problem is there's not a lot of guidance out there for people who just want to get started on their sustainable investing journey. The financial industry doesn't pay a great deal of attention to anyone who doesn't have big bucks to invest. And that's just plain wrong. The industry also does a fantastic job at putting people off, through ridiculous jargon and nonsensical terminology.

This sits at the heart of why I am focusing on women.

Of course, sustainable investing is not solely for women. Absolutely not. This has to be a collective effort and I genuinely hope that many men pick up this book too. But we do know that many women feel excluded from the financial industry, whether that is because of confidence, overuse of jargon that puts us off or simply the way the industry interacts with female clients. The feminist voice in me is shouting out that this has to change.

There's another important trend in there too – we have a pile of data telling us that many women are impassioned and inspired by issues of sustainability and that this extends to their financial decisions. Again, this isn't to the exclusion of men, but we need to bring it into focus.

It's time we pulled this all together so that we have something that speaks directly to women, in a field that is overly dominated by testosterone. The financial industry has done an excellent job at excluding many women and it's time we democratised it.

## WHEN YOU PUT THIS BOOK DOWN...

I want to connect you with the possibilities of what you can do. I want to give you goosebumps when you think about how smart you can be in the way you leverage the money, the wealth, you have.

By the end of the book I hope that you will feel like you could have a conversation about sustainable investing – with your friends, with your partner, with your parents. I want you to help me spread the word, have profound conversations about the future of money and what it can mean for us.

I also want you to be able to head to your bank or meeting with your financial advisor and confidently express what matters to you in terms of your investment decisions and not be patronised or fed misinformation. This is the moment when we stop getting pushed around.

Don't get me wrong – this book has limitations, and some important ones that you should be aware of. Sustainable investing is an emerging field, it's nascent, which means there is a lot of growing up that needs to be done. Especially for retail investors, women like you and me. My intention is to plant the initial seed, to outline what can be done and then to encourage you to take the next steps seeking more information and potentially guidance from a good investment professional.

I have also written this book very much with a global audience in mind, so please be aware that not every example is relevant to every country or every market.

There are huge geographical, commercial and regulatory differences that mean you may need to do some work to figure out what's happening on the ground where you manage your money.

## ALL THAT ASIDE

The sustainable investing world is in constant flux (hey, what isn't?). There is so much more to learn about what we can and can't do. The industry itself needs to do some serious soul searching. But if you are starting to have a strong pounding in your heart, if you feel that we can't keep watching the bad stuff happen, if your values are speaking louder and louder to you, it's worth taking some time to read on.

The bottom line is, if you are not involved with your money, you probably aren't thinking about the impact it has on our world. But money is power, and you have the power to choose where it goes, the impact it has. Take time to be informed, take time to join the movement.

You are not alone because there is a whole sisterhood out there figuring out how to do this. Please come join us. While I cannot promise an easy ride, it's one we can take together. And the sense of well-being that comes from knowing that your financial choices are aligned with your values, with the authentic you, is pretty powerful.

You don't need millions to start investing. And you certainly don't need millions to invest in alignment with what you believe in. My goal is simple: to begin empowering you with knowledge to start taking action. My goal is to bring as many women as possible into our movement so that we can use the levers we have at hand to demand a better world. My goal is to help you become a sustainable investor.

*Jessica Robinson, 2020*

# ONE

## MONEY, MONEY, MONEY – WOMEN AND THE THORNY ISSUE OF WEALTH

Money is a tricky topic and for many women it's almost taboo. Why is this? Why does it throw up so many different emotions, many of which are negative? I want to explore women's unique relationship with money – and the different drivers that sit behind this. Fortunately, there is increasing data on how women feel about and act on money, as well as their somewhat peculiar relationship with the financial industry. This is useful stuff because it can help us to figure out what we need to do better for women and their wealth.

It is likely that you are a woman – after all, you picked up a book subtitled *A Woman's Guide*! Yes – I am pitching this book at women, but at the same time, I do not want us to be fixated on a comparative discussion about women versus men. Sure, some comparison is interesting and, at times, illuminating. However, the intention behind focusing on women is not to engage in a tit-for-tat argument over what women do better or worse than men.

Rather, it is to recognise the uniqueness of where many women stand today when it comes to the thorny issue of wealth. It is to recognise that many women need solutions tailored to their specific needs and ambitions that, to date, haven't been fully addressed by the financial industry.

## WOMEN ARE HELD BACK WHEN IT COMES TO MONEY. PERIOD.

It's fair to say that women all over the world face a lot of challenges because they are, well, women. And this is never truer than when it comes to money and wealth. While somewhat of a generalisation, when you compare the financial positions of men against women you cannot help but be confounded by the extent to which women are not receiving their fair share on the money front. So, what's up?

Over recent years, there has been a huge amount of attention given to the gender pay gap – basically, the average difference in remuneration between men and women who are working. And rightly so. It's a critical and underpinning issue.

The World Economic Forum has reported that, at the slow speed experienced over the period 2006–20, the economic gender gap (the global 'Economic Participation and Opportunity gap') will take 257 years to close.[1] Why? Because it is so vast, and the pace of change is so slow.

But there's more. There are a whole host of other 'gaps' at play here and they all interact, overlap and pretty much change the game at the outset for most women. Ellevest, a US robo-advisor (robo-advisors are automated investment services or online advisors) designed especially for women, does a great job at categorising and explaining these gaps to us in its Mind the Gap Guide.[2] Here's what it identifies:

### Gender pay gap

The big one. Already defined above, there are a lot of different numbers out there and, of course, it varies from country to country, market to market. The International Labour Organization regularly produces a Global Wage Report, offering a more accurate way of calculating the gender pay gap, self-described as the 'factor weighted gender pay gap'. The Global Wage Report 2018/19 found that the global estimate stands at 20 per cent.[3] That means, as an estimate, men are earning 20 per cent more than women for comparative jobs. Which is just crazy.

### Gender work achievement gap

The Ellevest Guide describes this as: 'Besides being a mouthful, it's when we women fall behind in our careers while our male peers are promoted to positions of power.' I know I have experienced this and, while it is complex, I can think of multiple reasons as to why I have seen this occur, and it is rarely based on competency or talent.

### Gender debt gap

Yes, this is actually a thing. Why? Because women tend to pay more for their debt than men do, and women have more of certain types of debt than men. None of which is good for the debt position of women all over the world – we are simply in it more deeply.

## Gender investing gap

This comes about when women aren't investing at all and actually leaving much of their savings in cash. The purpose of this book is to show women how to avoid this trap, so we'll leave it there for now and come back to this issue later.

## Gender funding gap

Female-led businesses are receiving much less funding than male-led businesses. There are a lot of stats on how big the funding gap is but here's a good one which really highlights the size of the problem. According to data from PitchBook (a financial data and software provider based in Seattle), venture capital investment in all-female founding teams hit $3.3 billion in 2019, representing just 2.8 per cent of capital invested across the entire US startup ecosystem.[4] There's so much wrong with this number and if just reading this makes your blood boil as much as it does mine, you will enjoy later chapters on both gender-lens and angel investing, which aim to turn this around.

## Gender pricing gap

Basically this form of economic discrimination rears its ugly head when women get to the counter to discover they are paying more than men for the same products. Yes, I'm serious! Sometimes labelled the 'pink tax', examples include razors, clothing, dry cleaning, personal care products. It's quite a list.

## Unpaid labour gap

Unpaid labour is the chores we do at home. And yes, you guessed it, it seems that women do a whole lot more than men.

## Gender pension gap

As women, we seem to be facing many challenges but just to add another – a manifestation perhaps of the impact of all the gaps, and worthy of a callout on its own – and that is: *the gender pension gap* (or the retirement needs gap). This represents the percentage difference in pension income for female pensioners compared to male pensioners. Recent estimates are putting the global gender pension gap typically at an estimated 30–40 per cent.[5]

There are all sorts of reasons as to why women tend to be worse off in retirement than men. The obvious one is the pay gap, but women are also accumulating less wealth before they hit retirement age than men. This can be compounded by poor access to company pension schemes if women are not in full-time permanent employment.

At the same time, women are likely to need more money than men during retirement because they often live longer (therefore facing overall higher costs), live longer alone (and thus have no one to share living expenses with) and face higher healthcare costs (because they are less likely to have a spouse to take care of them so they must rely on professional carers during later life). It is almost a perfect storm.

Of course, the gender pension gap hits a woman at the worst time in life – when there is little that she can do about it. It is becoming a huge issue across the world. Take, for example, Europe – the difference in pension income between men and women is significant and yet there seems little agreement on what needs to be done to resolve it.[6] This problem isn't going away, so, as you think through your own financial plan and investment strategy, keep it in mind so that your retirement planning accurately reflects your unique needs and circumstances.

## BACK TO THE GENDER INVESTING GAP

Now let's get back to the gender investing gap as this sits at the core of this book. The harsh reality is that many women face a glaring gender investing gap – it is a major issue. Just take a look at some of the stats to bring home how big the problem is:

- In Australia, a report by Fidelity International (a company providing investment management services), *The financial power of women: A state of the nation report on the barriers to women investing*, found that over half of 815 women surveyed did not hold any savings products other than their superannuation (Australia's organisational pension fund scheme).[7] Less than half invested in shares and less than a quarter invested in a managed fund.[8]

- In the UK, a recent study from market research firm Kantar TNS identified that there is a £15 billion gender investment gap. In this nationally representative survey, it was found that men hold double the amount of investments held by women.[9]

- A US study by Prudential, *Financial Experience & Behaviors among Women*, found that 70 per cent of women consider themselves savers as opposed to investors. Yet 70 per cent of men said they enjoyed the 'sport of investing', being prepared to take on risk in order to earn greater financial reward.[10]

- When you look at who uses online investment platforms, we see similar trends. For example, at Interactive Investor, a UK online service, only 28 per cent of customers are women. At Wealthsimple, a Canadian-headquartered online investment service, it's only marginally higher at 33 per cent – and Wealthsimple offers events specifically targeting women.[11]

- Turning to Asia, a study of the gender retirement savings gap of women in a number of ASEAN (Association of South East Asian Nations) economies found that women on average have about 32 per cent lower savings – both on the personal and mandatory national levels.[12]

## WHY DOES THIS MATTER?

Women are not investing to the same extent as men, saving less for retirement and parking more in cash.

And this results in a significant financial shortfall in the longer term. Of course, the pay disparity compounds this shortfall, but it also means that women are missing out on making the money they do have work better for them. The result is that women have less wealth and are expecting to retire on much less than men. This matters when you look at the numbers – for example, in the UK, a woman's pension pot is expected to be two-thirds that of a man.[13]

In general, the stock market tends to do better than cash over the longer term. A woman could potentially earn higher financial returns by putting her wealth into, say, an equity fund. Take a look online for illustrations of what this could represent – some wealth managers give worked-out examples of the wealth you could have built if investing in a well-diversified portfolio versus a savings account over a given period.

Parking your wealth in cash may make you feel more secure; of course I understand that, particularly during these turbulent and challenging times. However, if you don't start actively investing your wealth, you may well be missing out on potential financial returns.

At the same time, you are also missing out on the opportunity to do something positive and constructive with it in terms of societal or environmental impact. If you actively invest you can choose to invest in sectors that you really want to see grow – such as clean energy or sustainable consumer brands – or proactively put your money into companies with strong records on environmental and social issues. The world is your oyster.

## WHAT IS HOLDING WOMEN BACK?

So why is the gender investment gap arising? Let's explore some of the reasons as to why we may not be investing as much as men. I will admit that it's a tricky one, with many gender stereotypes and assumptions floating around, so keep in mind that there is no black and white explanation here. These factors also overlap, feeding into one another as we travel through our financial and professional lives.

### Confidence

Research indicates that women lack confidence when it comes to investing, pushing them towards lower risk options such as cash savings accounts. Do read the report published by Fidelity International mentioned before, which found women's confidence is often hit because they don't feel they understand financial products well enough. A recent J.P. Morgan survey also found that the main factors hindering women are a lack of confidence, but also the lack of time and limited investment knowledge.[14]

For sure, it seems that to be cautious on investing is the default approach for many women. One has to wonder, though, if it is a self-fulfilling prophecy. If men are more likely to invest in stocks and shares, and with stock markets generally giving stronger returns over time, this means their investments are creating more value in the longer term. Let's assume the experience builds on men's confidence, while women move in the opposite direction.

## Language

There is plenty of research around how women feel about the conversations they have with financial and investment professionals about investing – and the findings are not good. Conversations about money can be intimidating. The language used by most finance bods is, at best, unfamiliar; at worst, utterly baffling; and, at times, condescending. And it gets even harder if you want to use your wealth to do some good (more on that later). So, it seems that the language the industry is using can be very off-putting to women when it comes to the investing game. What's worse, in a male-oriented financial industry, not much has been done to encourage female investing and build levels of financial literacy, certainly not until very recently.

## Perception

It is probably true that many of us do not actually consider ourselves to be investors in the first place. Which is crazy because, if we are investing through our workplace pensions, we already are! For some women, there is certainly a perception that investing is simply 'not for them', it's not an option. Perhaps this is compounded by all of the issues identified above – and in a world where, all too often, women are labelled as spenders versus men who are categorised as earners, it's no wonder we struggle to see ourselves as investors.

## Communication

It's not just the language and terminology used. It's the core messages we communicate to women when it comes to our money assumptions and expectations. And you can see where our self-image that we are 'not investors' comes from.

For example, fantastic research from Starling Bank, an upstart in the UK banking scene, looked at 300 articles and found that the way we communicate with men and women about finances is very different.[15] Women were defined as 'excessive spenders' across 65 per cent of the articles targeting them. They were given guidance to 'limit, restrict and take better control of shopping splurges', with 71 per cent of articles encouraging them to seek discounts and bargains to save money. Articles aimed at men used language such as 'dare' to encourage men to 'invest', with implications that financial successes made readers 'more of a man'.

## DO WOMEN INVEST DIFFERENTLY TO MEN? AND DOES IT MATTER?

I'm honestly not sure if the question of whether women and men invest differently really matters in the grand scheme of things, but it's quite interesting to explore the different ways in which it might manifest. At the very least, we can dispel any unnecessary stereotypes and examine how some of the barriers we note above actually play into how a woman may or may not invest.

## Risk tolerance

Of course, not everyone (woman or man) will manage their money in the same way. In particular, different people view risk in different ways. There has been quite a strong view that there are notable differences between women and men when it comes to risk. For example, a Wells Fargo Investment Institute study of US investors found that 16 per cent of men identify as 'more aggressive' compared to just 4 per cent of women.[16] Research from financial services provider Aegon showed that, in the UK, 17 per cent of men say they are comfortable with taking risks with their money, compared to just 6 per cent of women.[17] I still remain to be convinced that it is as black and white as this and I wonder if risk tolerance levels will shift rapidly as women become more financially confident.

## Financial goals

Some commentators argue that women tend to be more relational with their wealth, less driven by processes and results. The observation that women tend to integrate their financial goals with their career and family goals could also indicate that high financial returns and 'beating the benchmark' are less significant for some women.[18] Research tells us that wealth for many women is about providing for family, security and comfort.[19] I suppose we could describe this as women seeing the bigger picture and how this calls on them to consider their financial goals in conjunction with broader life goals.

### Time to make decisions

When women make a decision, they tend to want more time, to look at more information and to be more thorough than men. This may hold particularly true when it comes to financial and investment decisions, which can require more in-depth consideration.

### Levels of financial literacy

Unfortunately, it seems that women score lower than men on financial literacy measures. For example, the Global Financial Literacy Excellence Center found that, globally, 35 per cent of men are financially literate compared with 30 per cent of women, and that this trend is found in both advanced and emerging economies.[20] This can negatively impact women's long-term financial well-being, particularly because financial literacy has been linked to wealth accumulation, stock market participation and retirement planning, which is clearly tied up in the factors holding female would-be investors back.

## DO THESE DIFFERENCES MAKE WOMEN WORSE INVESTORS?

Of course not. And in fact, it appears that the myth that women aren't as good investors is just that. A myth. The evidence is stacking up that women are in fact good investors. For example:

- UK investment platform Hargreaves Lansdown found that, over three years, its female clients saw the value of their investments grow by 0.81 per cent more than men.[21] This may not sound a lot but – based on those numbers – over 30 years, women would end up with 25 per cent more than men.

- Fascinating research by Warwick Business School found that while annual returns on investments for men were on average a marginal 0.14 per cent above the performance of the FTSE 100, annual returns on the investment portfolios held by women were 1.94 per cent above it.[22] Basically, this means that returns for women investing outperformed men by 1.8 per cent.

- Despite evidence to the contrary, Fidelity Investments found that only 9 per cent of women believe that they are more capable than men when it comes to investing.[23]

The message in all of this is that women are far better investors than they think. When we look at women who actually are investing, they clearly are doing it well and make savvy investment decisions. You could also argue that their commitment to not taking excessive risk could play a role in why they may be such good investors.

## WOMEN AND THE FINANCIAL INDUSTRY

All of these factors point to a systemic problem within the financial industry which is seemingly either not understanding or simply excluding women. This is reflected in research from EY that found that 75 per cent of women feel misunderstood by wealth managers.[24] Based on bitter personal experience, I can see how that might be the case!

Most financial companies are treating women and men more or less in the same way. But we're not the same. Chances are we're earning 20 per cent less than most men and that's just the pay gap. Many women take time out of the workforce to care for children or ageing parents, some returning to work on a part-time basis resulting in them earning less and saving less. Women are likely to live six to eight years longer, outliving their saved capital and perhaps facing steeper long-term care costs. These differences are stark and yet we are still struggling to reflect this in our approaches to retirement planning and in the financial industry more broadly.

The financial industry plays a huge role in how women interact with money and how they approach investing. The world of finance has been heavily dominated by men and a male way of thinking. Over the last decade or so, this has certainly begun to change. For example, there is a lot of talk about gender equality within financial institutions, promoting more women to higher levels of management and bringing in better diversity policies.

Unfortunately, there is also a 'but' as these efforts are limited. Just take a look at the glaring gender pay gaps that continue at some of the world's top banks. In the UK, a recent report by Reuters showed that major financial services firms had made very little progress in narrowing the gap between male and female pay. Shockingly, more than a third had actually gone backwards.[25]

Despite women having increasing influence as consumers, in fact more than ever before, our financial needs continue not to be met. The crazy thing is that it makes good business sense to change this. Oliver Wyman, the consulting firm, recently published research that argued financial services companies can generate more than $700 billion in additional revenues every year if they take steps to better understand what their female clients need.[26]

There is a lot we could say about the role that women play in the industry, but I want to pick up on two themes in particular:

## 1. Women as customers and how the financial services industry communicates with them

It's no surprise that, given the male dominance of the industry, the marketing and communication efforts of the big financial institutions have not really reflected that a large part of their customer base is female. Sure, we are seeing more and more campaigns aimed at women. But it's more nuanced than this.

It is not simply about recognising that women are customers or simply feminising financial products. It's about being aware of the attitudinal differences that women have when making investment decisions and developing communications that take these into account. This means focusing on how women take more time to reach financial decisions as well as conferring with experts or their peers and understanding that women have a different relationship with money and the concept of wealth.

On top of this, we've also got to appreciate that women are not a homogeneous group. This means appreciating their differences as well as how their needs change at different stages of life. All of this is central to connecting with women and truly delivering services and products that fit with what they are looking for.

We've got a lot of work to do. Many women feel that the financial industry treats them in a condescending or patronising way. So let's call it out, let's pressure the industry to do better by women. It seems to me that it is the right time to challenge traditional and outdated assumptions, and to push for an industry that reflects the needs of a growing female customer base.

---

**CHARLOTTE WILKINSON, FOUNDER, HELLO SISTER**

*Hello Sister is a women-focused brand and marketing consultancy, serving clients in their female-focused insight, communications, innovation and strategy needs.*

**Why are financial brands struggling with how to communicate with their female customers?**

We know that women are not homogeneous, with many of us wearing many 'persona hats' at the same time. Sometimes it is hard for many brands to try and connect with women effectively without being condescending.

However, one of the main challenges is that beyond demographic and financial data, financial institutions know very little about their female customers and targets, so tend to target them only through the lenses of data they have – for example, a high-net-worth woman or a young mother. This results in much of the communications being generic at best, allowing no leeway for expertise, knowledge, attitudinal or behavioural differences. At worst, it comes across as patronising when you are telling a female business owner who happens to also be a mother and shopping lover how she can be savvy with her money, for example.

While we know the financial industry is making efforts to understand its female client base better, there is still a long way to go. An important part of this is getting more women into the industry and the decision-making structures of the financial world. Quite often we are still collecting data through a male lens and this needs to be addressed, along with understanding the nuances of the different roles a woman plays.

## 2. Women as employees in the financial industry

There has been a lot of noise around gender diversity in the financial industry and for infinite good reasons. Again, it's probably no surprise that progress has been slow and there is still a long, long road to travel. A couple more stats for you:

- In 2018, there were 191 men and 41 women in the top teams of the 20 leading financial services companies. Globally this represents an increase of female leaders from 13 per cent in 2014 to 18 per cent in 2018 – but wow, still only 18 per cent! And regional differences are huge – for example, in Asia only 6 per cent of senior executives are women, compared with 33 per cent in the US.[27]

- Let's look at the investment industry more specifically. Morningstar, the US-based investment research firm, tracks the progress of women working in the fund management industry globally. It found that, at the end of 2000, 14 per cent of fund managers were women. And at the end of 2019, 14 per cent of fund managers were women.[28] No progress at all.

## DIVERSITY AND ADVANCING THE FINANCIAL INDUSTRY TO BETTER DELIVER FOR ALL

Diversity of thought, experience and action are important for the financial industry to be able to telegraph and avoid risks, such as those that contributed to the global financial crisis. Many observers argue that this was borne from complacency and unacceptable risk taking. You may well have heard the famous words from Christine Lagarde, then Head of the International Monetary Fund (IMF): 'If it had been Lehman Sisters rather than Lehman Brothers, the world might well look a lot different today.'[29]

The push for greater gender diversity within the financial industry will bring positive change to its nuts and bolts, which in turn will hopefully ensure that the financial needs of women are better understood and served. At the same time, our drive for gender equality will bring broader benefits across our financial systems, markets and economies. For example, just take a look at the findings from the IMF which identified that narrowing the gender gap would foster greater stability in the banking systems and promote economic growth, as well as contribute to more effective fiscal and monetary policy.[30] The writing is on the wall, right?

As a final point, I want to make it clear that we are not only talking about gender diversity. We are talking about all types of diversity – for example, diversity of race, ethnicity, sexual orientation, age and so on. If we are aiming for financial inclusion, whereby all people are represented, we urgently need to address this – after all, it's completely rational for people seeking financial advice to feel that they are understood and represented. It's completely rational for customers to want financial institutions to understand and reflect in their products and services the differing needs of people.

### MANDY KIRBY, CHIEF STRATEGIST, CITY HIVE

*City Hive is an independent body focused on changing the culture of the investment management industry to ensure greater inclusion, diversity and equality.*

**Why is it important that we have more women in financial services?**

Research is increasingly showing there are real business benefits to having diversity of representation in senior leadership and across the business. From the point of view of the company, a failure to address diversity means they are missing out on talent. The short-term effects of this may not be easy to see, but over the long term, they will have failed to future-proof their organisation.

The world has changed. Microfinance has long understood that empowering women leads to better financial outcomes for the family and often the village, where investments are made into local businesses that create sustainable income. Now, women are increasingly demanding that they are properly catered for. For a long time, the views of women have been undervalued as well as the impact of decisions on their lives and livelihoods.

Across mainstream investment, there is often a misunderstanding of the real day-to-day financial decisions that women have to make. Understanding these pressures – especially the one that means women under-invest in their pensions in order to meet immediate needs – will help transform financial security for women.

And any efforts to rebuild trust, design new products, rethink investment practices will be undermined without more women in financial services, because we need to be able to see women everywhere, and in all roles, to be able to take the focus of the tiny handful of examples we currently have. Even the inspirational CEOs and leaders we have are expected to carry the burden of speaking for or representing all women, when in fact they are just individual humans. So role models – or, as is becoming more common, 'real models' – are really important.

### What do we need to do to bring more women into the industry?

We're looking for a paradigm shift in the asset and investment industry. To address the imbalance of women, a number of structural factors must be addressed. This starts with teaching children about money and finance as a core subject so that we see more young women studying finance – we know that, and we know it takes time. However, companies that are able to embrace changes to the way they work, to allow flexibility and balance, will be able to attract and retain a broader range of clients that feel their needs are understood and are being met.

# TWO

# ENOUGH ALREADY – IT'S
# TIME FOR CHANGE

Looking at the extensive analysis that now exists on women and their relationship with money, one thing is clear – something needs to change and pretty damn quickly. There are multiple gaps we have to work hard to close and we have a lot to shout about to push for equality.

How are we going to get there? A great deal is happening, all around the world, and the emergence of the concept of 'financial feminism' is front and centre of these efforts. In this chapter, we explore what this means, to us as women grappling with our money, and how it is hugely welcome by providing us with a focus through which we can push for change. But I contend that we are missing a beat if we don't use this momentum to ask deeper questions – does financial feminism simply mean that women close some of the gaps we have identified? Or can it mean something more? Can it mean that women determine how wealth is directed, that women recalibrate the concept of investing and value? I believe so.

# ENTER NOW, FINANCIAL FEMINISM

To me, the concept of financial feminism is deeply inspiring – on both a personal and a professional level. I genuinely believe we can take powerful strides forward by recognising the importance of what financial feminism is demanding, but also the solutions needed to address these demands. Financial feminism has shaped much of my world-view in recent years and encapsulates a great deal of the reasoning behind my passion for writing this book. It represents an opportunity for real and fundamental change – and this truly excites me.

## Laying the context for financial feminism

What are we talking about when we use the term 'financial feminism'? As with all things related to feminism, we are talking about equality – in this case, the belief in the financial equality of women. The whole concept is rapidly gathering interest and momentum across the world, as we wake up to the challenges that many women face when it comes to money. As we've already figured out – these are multiple, complex and huge.

I have some reluctance about labels, but I can't help but love this one. Why? Because it's driving specific conversations around women and money. And these are conversations we need to have. They are also conversations that should be empowering because they have the potential to provide us with the freedom of choice and the power to direct our lives, careers, families – and everything, really.

**What does it mean to be a financial feminist today?**
There are so many important aspects to the current debate
on feminism and it is not the purpose of this book to
describe or dissect these individually. However, it is our
job to talk about how financial feminism sits at the core
of many of these aspects and identify what it can mean
for women now. You may well have heard this wonderful
quote from Gloria Steinem, often dubbed 'the world's
most famous feminist', who so succinctly stated: 'We will
never solve the feminisation of power until we solve the
masculinity of wealth.'

To be a financial feminist is to believe that women have
a right to financial equality. It also requires that one talks,
acts and advocates to make this happen. For all women.

How do we do this?

1. View our financial health in the same way we view
   self-care – it's really important for our long-term well-
   being. So, make it a priority and encourage other
   women in your life to do the same.
2. Push for change in the workplace – where female
   employees are not being treated in the same way as
   male colleagues, call it out. Of course, this has a lot to
   do with pay parity, but it also relates to other company
   policies such as parental leave or flexible working
   hours, as well as bonus and work pension schemes.
3. Talk about money so that it is no longer considered
   a taboo – be open about it, with girlfriends, sisters,
   daughters, mothers. Empower one another by sharing

your knowledge and experience, encourage each and every woman you know to take control and talk openly about the challenges they face.

4. Use your wealth to support other women – we've got a whole chapter on gender-lens investing, but it's so important to flag it here too. We've seen the gender funding gap – let's do something about it today.

If we are aiming for financial equality and independence for women, then we also need to focus on how women can develop not only the right investing skills, but also investing confidence. Investing isn't just a man's game.

## Don't just invest more, invest more consciously

It's pretty exciting, right? Financial feminism is a thing... and more and more women are getting behind it.

But this is where I want to slow down the excitement and ask you if we are missing something really important here? As we leverage the interest in financial feminism to address both the gender pay and gender investing gaps, we also have the opportunity to talk about HOW women want to use their money.

We can also begin to have conversations about how financial feminism is not just about getting women to invest more. It is also about empowering women to invest in the type of future they want to build. I believe this is a really big opportunity and, if we can make it fly, we are at a point in time where we can build a movement, one where a financial feminist is someone who uses her wealth to build a more sustainable, cleaner and fairer world. To me, this is where the real excitement – and ultimately empowerment – sits.

Put simply, if there is one thing you need to take away from this book, financial feminism is not just about women earning and investing on a par with men. Financial feminism represents the opportunity for women to use their financial power to build the kind of world that they want to live in. Financial feminism gives women a voice to determine how the world should change for the better.

## A WORLD IN CRISIS – THE SUSTAINABILITY CHALLENGES WE FACE

And the world does need changing for the better. From where many of us stand, our collective future is looking bleak. We are sitting on the brink of a climate and environmental crisis; inequalities (whether these be financial or educational, or access to basic healthcare or other services to address needs) are widening; large corporates continue to turn a blind eye to the root causes of unsavoury practices such as child labour, modern slavery or human trafficking in supply chains; corruption and abuse are still widespread; and women and girls remain woefully behind on any equality scale. In many ways, the COVID-19 pandemic accentuated these problems, illustrating, perhaps in the starkest way possible, how interconnected yet how divided we are. In unpredictable and widescale global shocks such as this, those who suffer the most are those who have the least.

For the purpose of this book, let's call these 'sustainability challenges'. When you look at some of the numbers, it really tells you how devastating the situation is. For example:

- According to the Credit Suisse Global Wealth Report, the world's richest 1 per cent, those with more than $1 million, own 44 per cent of the world's wealth. Their data also shows that adults with less than $10,000 in wealth make up 56.6 per cent of the world's population but hold less than 2 per cent of global wealth.[1]

- In the world's poorest countries, slightly more than one in four children are engaged in child labour. These children are too young to work or are involved in hazardous activities that impact on their mental, educational and physical development.[2]

- Worldwide, an estimated 650 million girls and women alive today were married before their 18th birthday. Globally, the total number of girls married in childhood is estimated at 12 million per year.[3]

- In 2017, one in three girls aged 15 to 19 had been subjected to female genital mutilation in the 30 countries where the practice is concentrated.[4]

- The United Nations released a landmark report in 2019 which reported that one in four premature deaths and diseases worldwide are due to man-made pollution and environmental damage.[5]

- Our throwaway culture means that every year we dump a massive 2.12 billion tonnes of waste. To think about this in reality, if we put all that waste on trucks, they could go around the world 24 times.[6]

- Climate change… well, I think everyone reading this book knows how seriously devastating this is. But do you know how disproportionately climate change affects women? For example, UN figures indicate that 80 per cent of people displaced by climate change are women. Despite this, the average representation of women in national and global climate negotiating bodies sits below 30 per cent.[7]

As I researched these numbers, I couldn't help but well up with tears. We have been grappling with these challenges for a long, long time – way back to the 1980s when the concept of sustainable development first emerged. The Brundtland Commission was appointed in 1983, by the then United Nations Secretary-General Javier Pérez de Cuéllar, with the mission of uniting countries to figure out how to pursue sustainable development together as a collective. It was a very important point in time because it gave us a global agreement, a common language, on sustainable development.

The Brundtland Commission finally agreed on a definition: 'Sustainable development is development that meets the needs of the present, without compromising the ability of future generations to meet their own needs.'

A great deal of this was driven by a concern about the rapid deterioration of our natural world and depletion of our natural resources. The journey from then to now charts many different agreements, treaties and actions. Some successes but also a lot of failures.

Today we are beginning to face up to these failures because the realities we face are forcing conversations about where we are going wrong. The Sustainable Development Goals (SDGs; covered in much detail in Chapter 6) are partly a response to this. The problem is we are way off target in hitting the SDGs and there is much more that needs to be done. Something needs to change – and this is where sustainable investing is important. Because money matters, and money plays a pivotal role.

## Why does money matter?

Why is this the case, why does money matter in all of this? Antony Bugg-Levine, the original impact investing pioneer, explained this so simply when he said:

> Money is a construct. Humans came up with it. It was a way to organise our economy in our societies, but it's not an end in itself. It really has always been a means to create the world that we want to live in.[8]

Yes. Money – and its place in the world, the way we use it to measure and translate value – can be transformative if we choose to make it so. The private sector and profit-oriented companies have a role to play in figuring out how to solve many of the environmental and social problems we face.

As investors, we can put our money into companies and sectors that are aligned with our sustainability values and beliefs – for example, companies that consider their environmental footprint and take action to reduce it; companies that have strong labour practices and protect their employees; and companies that are open and transparent in the way that they operate. In this way, we can, as Bugg-Levine says, create the world that we want to live in.

I find it heartening that we are having more and more dialogue about what role businesses and companies could and should play in building our future, a future that is fit for all people. It is an exciting discussion and I really urge you to play a part yourself. But first, let's get back to the sisterhood and two important trends that make this call on financial feminism so pressing.

## THE TWO TRENDS THAT MATTER

There's a great deal of data and research out there on investment trends and practices. However, until fairly recently this was limited when it came to coverage on either:

1. women as investors per se

or

2. female investors' thinking and preferences on sustainable investing.

The good news is that over the last few years this has begun to change substantially. Why? Well, because the financial industry has seen the writing on the wall. To put it bluntly, these two major trends signal massive market opportunities for the industry.

**First, money is no longer just a man's game**

Women are rapidly taking their rightful place as economic powerhouses. We own more and more of the wealth, whether we earn it, inherit it or it comes from divorce. This trend is occurring across the globe and it represents a huge potential market for wealth managers. Here are some of the numbers:

- By 2015, it was estimated that women held 30 per cent of global private wealth, which was a scaling up from previous numbers. From that point onwards it was expected that their wealth would grow by 7 per cent annually.[9]

- By 2018, Credit Suisse reported in its Global Wealth Report that this actually stood at 40 per cent once non-financial assets (assets that cannot be traded on the financial markets such as land, vehicles, etc.) had been included. These make up half of global household wealth and are shared more equally between women and men.

- More women are entering the economic mainstream for the first time as consumers, producers, entrepreneurs and employees. It is expected that women will control close to 75 per cent of discretionary spending worldwide by 2028.[10]

There are of course large regional differences, but most trends see women's share of wealth rising considerably.

- In Australia, women have dramatically increased their wealth relative to men – in 2007, men held an average of 27.4 per cent more wealth than women; this advantage decreased to 12.3 per cent in 2019.[11] The gap seems to be closing.

- 53 per cent of UK millionaires will be female by 2025, according to the Centre for Economics and Business Research.[12]

- In China, Credit Suisse estimates women's wealth share to be between 30 per cent and 40 per cent. Of particular note is the number of Chinese women making the global rich listings – there are a fair few women on the billionaires' rankings, according to Bloomberg, Forbes and their Chinese counterpart Hurun.

All of this is fantastic because it means women – finally – have a seat at the decision-making table. Actually, scrap that – women have the potential to build their own table. With these numbers moving in one direction, the influence and power that come with financial wealth are increasingly significant.

## Second, women are genuinely worried about the state of the world

Not only are many women genuinely worried about the

state of the world, they are thinking through how their financial and, in particular, investment decisions can have a positive impact. There's genuine interest in how we are investing our money.

I have known this instinctively for a few years now. In various roles and guises, I have been privileged to speak at many conferences and seminars on sustainable investing and other related topics like green finance. Many of these were at mainstream finance events and, while the room was heavily male-dominated, I was always struck by the disproportionate number of women who would approach me afterwards to talk further, take my business card and communicate how much my messages resonated with them.

This got me thinking – is there something more in this? Why are so many women drawn to this discussion? And so passionately? So, I began to research and discovered, while there wasn't a huge amount of data out there, there was sufficient evidence to indicate something was going on.

I decided to undertake my own research project through Moxie Future – an online platform and blog I had set up in my spare time, specifically to connect with women on these issues. We set about interviewing women in five countries – Australia, China, Germany, the USA and the UK. First, we wanted to get a sense for whether or not the anecdotal evidence was uncovering a bigger truth. Second, we wondered whether there were any regional or national differences in the way that women felt about investing and the impact they could have. This could potentially uncover what might drive these motivations and inform what we could do to encourage more of it.

So, what did we find?

A lot of women, in different countries, really care about where their money is invested – 83 per cent of women surveyed, in fact. Meanwhile, 79 per cent of women felt that we urgently need to act in order to build a better world for the future. And a whopping 69 per cent felt it was important that their investment and savings decisions should reflect their personal values and philosophies.

These findings are reflected in other research. For example, a US study by Morgan Stanley Institute for Sustainable Investing found that women (84 per cent) were more receptive to sustainable investing than men (67 per cent).[13] Another previous study by the same organisation had found that female investors were nearly twice as likely as male investors to consider both the rate of return and the positive impact made by a company when making an investment. In another example, Calvert Investments found, in its study of affluent women, that 95 per cent ranked 'helping others' and 90 per cent ranked 'environmental responsibility' as important.[14] Interesting stuff.

## There's no stopping us

You take these two significant trends and you can see why I get so excited about the potential to create a movement here, right? Women are owning more of the world's wealth and women are clearly driven and motivated to do more with this wealth. This is huge. Women care. Yes, they care about the state of the world. They care about where their money goes. They care about the companies and sectors they invest in. Not just a little bit, but a lot.

## So why aren't we doing more (yet)?

Moxie Future's research confirmed that women face a number of complex and interrelated barriers. And they're largely the same barriers that prevent women from investing in the first place. While many women want to act as sustainable investors, they are often held back by a lack of time, a lack of confidence or a lack of understanding on how to get started. Sometimes, actually most of the time, all three.

With the financial industry already not doing a great job at serving women, this becomes accentuated when female investors are looking to follow a path that is different from the norm. During the course of our research we found that many women continue to feel talked down to or misunderstood by (mostly male) financial advisors, often bombarded with meaningless financial jargon and concepts. Banks are no better, often telling a female client that they can only help if she has millions in assets. I tried this myself with my own, very well-known international bank, which told me that it could only talk to me about sustainable investing options through the private bank, which would require I hold $5 million in assets. Thanks.

The world is fundamentally changing. Both in terms of the pressing priorities we face but also the way in which we can solve them. In light of this, why should sustainable investing be the purview of the ultra-rich alone? Surely everyone should be able to determine where their money is invested, being empowered to make those decisions on the basis of her own knowledge and values?

Let's make this an exciting reality for any wealth-creating woman (in fact, any person) so that they can start to invest sustainably if they choose to. It's not a straightforward road, nor a smooth journey, but it's becoming an easier one to follow with fewer bumps along the way. As we travel, our challenge, and our opportunity, is to make it as easy as possible for others too. The investment industry, the wealth management sector, is ripe for disruption and hopefully this disruption will mean democratisation for the investing world – so that all women, all people, can direct their wealth towards the businesses that they want to support.

## MORE ABOUT THIS BOOK

This book is aimed at a broad church, to touch the hearts and minds of any women who are making, or looking to make, decisions over where to put their money. Its purpose is to be a springboard from which to get involved with the financial feminist movement. To take this one step further: to use this book to make change today.

Sure, this book is about helping women to think about investing in the first place, but it's also telling you that this alone is not enough. Financial feminism is not simply about investing more, it's about digging deeper and thinking about where you are investing.

## What will you get from this book?

Intended as a practical and accessible guide for all women, this book will:

- Offer plain-talking content about what sustainable investing is. This will include its history and development to date, the context within the broader world and what to expect in the future, as we are anticipating rapid change.

- Explain the link between the investment decisions we make and the societal and environmental transformations we want to see. In particular, we will explore the concept of capital and its purpose in the world today.

- Provide guidance on how to get started, how to take the first steps in aligning your money with your values and beliefs. This will include lots of definitions, suggestions and potential approaches that you will want to consider.

- Demystify some of the terms and jargon that dominate the financial services industry and explain how these relate to sustainable investing. Having some of the basics under your belt will help you take the next step in seeking advice from a qualified investment professional. It will build your confidence and help you deflect comments from the usual crowd of naysayers.

- Provide examples and case studies of women who have begun the sustainable investing journey, sharing their experiences and learnings from along the way. There is a tribe out there – you will be joining them!

## How to use this book effectively

There is a lot of information in these pages, even more if you follow up the endnotes and read further, so give yourself plenty of time to consider what matters to you and what doesn't matter. Sustainable investing is very personal because it is a reflection of who you are and the values you have. For this reason, there is no cookie-cutter approach. Rather you have to explore your own priorities and how these translate into the companies and sectors you want to invest in.

- Part I (chapters 3 to 6) gives you an introduction to what we are talking about and should leave you well positioned to take the next step.

- Part II (chapters 7 to 9) moves into practical guidance and this may be where you want to work through one chapter at a time, completing the self-analysis and conferring with friends, family and professionals.

- Part III (chapters 10 to 12) covers some specific areas that may or may not be of interest – indeed, you may want to take these one chapter at a time depending on whether it piques your interest or not.

The book draws to a conclusion in Chapter 13 by encouraging you to see that it doesn't stop here. This is just the beginning of the journey. There is much we can do, not only to move forward ourselves, but also to bring many others along with us. We can also play a huge role in changing the financial industry by using our voices to shout and shout loudly. When the industry players hear that people want something better, that their customers are not happy with the way things currently work, we will facilitate change. By telling financial advisors and banks that sustainability and impact matters, one day they will wake up. We can also choose to support the disruptors who are throwing curveballs at the traditional business models – if, like me, you are a rebel deep down, read on.

### SHARING SOME OF MY OWN JOURNEY

We know that there is a large proportion of women who think we need to act urgently to create a better world for tomorrow. We have the evidence. And I am proud to say that I am one of these women. But I struggled for a very long time over how to do something meaningful, beyond my work, beyond how I influenced my children and beyond what I bought (or didn't buy) in the supermarket or elsewhere.

When I was younger, I had money stashed in various bank accounts – current and savings – not doing much at all. I also had a couple of investment products that I'd gone into, thinking I needed to do more with my money, as well as various corporate pension plans from earlier in my career. At this point, I honestly believed, because I had been told in so many words by my own bank, that what I had was too small and this made me insignificant as a potential investor. It took me some time to realise that I could be a trailblazer.

I simply needed to overcome the limiting self-perception that I didn't have the wealth or the capabilities to do more. Once I did this, I was raring to go and genuinely excited to apply my smarts and my passion to do more with my money.

By definition, sustainable investing involves thinking about the environmental and social impact of your investment decisions, not simply focusing on financial returns. Learning that this was a possibility was a big game-changer for me in terms of how I understood my wealth. I began to think about the things that I am personally worried about. For me, I get seriously stressed about how slowly we are moving to combat climate change. I worry about who it will affect first – indeed, about the people it already has had a devastating impact on. It is these people who are already struggling day to day, the people who don't have the voice or the resources to respond or cope. I am determined that my money can be put to good use – not just for my own investment needs, but to address the needs of others at the same time.

For this reason, I am urgently looking to invest in companies and sectors that provide us with climate solutions and build climate resilience. The first thing I am staying away from is the fossil fuel industry – this industry is at the core of so much that is wrong with our world and the energy imbalances we face. I've been through what I am currently invested in to confirm whether or not any of the funds are big players in the sector and I've opted for the 'green funds' in my corporate pension plans. That said, there's a lot of 'greenwashing' out there so the due diligence needs to be done. It's a work in progress.

My next big personal project is to move investments into the clean energy sector. From a moral perspective, this just feels right. But from a financial and economic perspective, it has to be a smart move when we look at rising energy needs and how these cannot be fulfilled from burning more coal and oil, given the climate change commitments our governments made in the Paris Agreement. I have several economics degrees under my belt, including one in environmental economics, so I am convinced about the importance of this sector. While the research takes a bit of time, I am enjoying the learning and exploring the various clean energy investment funds that I might have access to.

## OLIVIA SIBONY, HEAD OF SEEDTRIBE IMPACT INVESTMENT

*SeedTribe Impact Investment is a spinoff of the UK's Angel Investment Network. SeedTribe is a community that connects the most exciting impactful start-ups with people who want to invest their time, energy or money. Angel Investment Network connects UK entrepreneurs and angel investors.*

**Based on what you see through your work with SeedTribe, to what extent do women think about sustainability and impact?**

I've been thrilled to see the higher proportion of women signing up to support profit-with-purpose businesses on SeedTribe, compared to our parent platform Angel Investment Network, which is sector-agnostic. A large number of women reach out to me on a regular basis as they are keen to get involved, wanting to support mission-driven businesses through their money, time and/or skills. It's been great to see this increase in activity in a space where traditionally fewer women are involved (the impact and start-up space).

**What might be holding female investors back from doing more in the sustainable investing space?**

Reports show that women tend to invest less than men, at all stages of investment. Start-ups do also present an additional risk compared to other investments. So, as a lot of work is being done to encourage more women to invest, the first challenge is getting them to focus on the safer investments such as pensions. Investing in pensions is important and there's huge potential to effect large-scale change with sustainable pensions investments, so this is something that should be actively promoted to everyone but may particularly appeal to women.

In addition to investing in sustainable pension funds, there's also a great opportunity to diversify portfolios with women becoming more involved in the sustainable start-up space, where they can invest some of their capital but also help mentor these businesses in order to help shape and scale them. There is therefore an opportunity to invest not just money but also time, using their skillsets to help shape the way businesses can grow and have a greater impact on people and planet, while being financially attractive.

**What can be done to support them on their sustainable investment journey?**

Creating networks to enable women to learn together, share their knowledge and varied skillsets in order to better understand the industry will help them take a more active part in this. By providing opportunities for collaboration, we can really help women be the drivers of the change we are starting to see in the world.

There's also a great opportunity for a paradigm shift. Instead of framing investments around the goal of financial return, we can show women that our money is our biggest and most direct vote for how the world is run. If we spend and invest our money wisely, ethically, sustainably, we are investing in the future of our world while also making sure we are looking into getting a good financial return on our investment. For example, by being proactive in ensuring we are investing our pensions sustainably – such as into renewable energies – we are reducing our long-term dependencies on oil, which is surely a safe bet both for our planet and for our wallets in the long term. Equally, investing into start-ups that help reduce carbon emissions will contribute to our reduction of harmful emissions but should also provide a good financial return if the technology is right.

We can apply this frame of mind not just to our long-term investments, but also to how we spend our money every day: buying more consciously – buying more durable items that are better sourced and create less waste at the end of their shelf-life – is a way to directly invest in people and the planet on a daily basis. The less harm we contribute to through our everyday patterns, the less we'll have to spend cleaning up the mess in the future, thus also providing a long-term financial benefit. So, investing sustainably should be a habit we form in our daily lives as well as our investments into financial products that help protect us for the long term. I believe it's not only an opportunity we all have, but a duty that we have if we are to leave this planet in a shape that we are proud of, for our future generations.

# PART I

# THREE

# WELCOME TO THE WONDERFUL WORLD OF INVESTING – COVERING OFF THE BASICS

Before I dive into the details of sustainable investing, let's talk more broadly about investing. In this chapter I will run through the basics – discussing the difference between saving and investing, some of the nitty-gritty concepts and terms you should be aware of, and then how this is translated into the different kinds of investment channels or 'asset classes' that may be available to you as an investor.

As you work your way through these pages, take some time to think about what investing actually represents – to you as an individual, for others as members of societies, for the varied actors that play a role in our markets and economies, and, of course, for the world as a whole.

This is an important thought process to go through, because it touches on a number of deep and philosophical questions which we perhaps need to explore as we contend with our ever-changing world. In particular, as we determine how to push forward with increasingly limited resources and widening inequalities on many fronts. Some of the questions you might want to ask yourself include:

- What is the real purpose of capital? Of wealth?

- What do we look for when we commit financial wealth to certain projects or businesses?

- What role does the corporate world play in our economies and societies?

- Should a company have a social conscience and, if so, societal responsibilities?

- How can we define what these responsibilities might be?

- How do we measure a company's performance against these commitments?

It's highly likely that, if you are reading this book, you have an understanding of what the term 'investing' means. Likewise, with the term 'capital'. This chapter is not intended to patronise you (particularly if you already know your stuff) or replace proper education on investing (specifically if you don't). Rather, the aim of this chapter is to cover just the basics to ensure that we are all on the same page before we move headfirst into the field of sustainable investing.

## JARGON BUSTING

There is just so much jargon flying around in the world of finance. Much of the industry continues to talk in riddles and many people (both men and women) find it all incredibly confusing, not to mention intimidating. It certainly makes it so much harder to know what you are investing in, or to understand the financial products you are buying, or even whether you are making the right decision, with any level of confidence.

Take it from me, the jargon and confusing terminology are by-and-large masking fairly straightforward concepts. Try not to let it put you off, because it shouldn't. The cynic in me often wonders if it has been designed this way to keep the masses out – perhaps this is another reason why the financial industry is ripe for democratisation.

## BACK TO BASICS

### The difference between saving and investing

It might be stating the obvious but there is a difference between saving and investing. Saving is quite simply income not spent. In other words, by putting money aside you are deferring some kind of consumption (some kind of future purchase) to a later time. You may choose to save with a bank (through a savings account) or look to other savings schemes or products that support your savings goals. In both circumstances the saver will earn interest – money paid regularly at a particular rate, usually being the current interest rate, which is quoted on an annual basis. Recently, interest rates on savings accounts have been historically low but this changes with bigger external factors such as the demand for money, reflecting whether an economy is growing or not.

Investing is a different beast altogether. Investing is putting your money into an asset or product with the goal of generating an income. This money is also called capital.[1] When it comes to investing and assets, in the finance world (the one we are talking about now), these assets are monetary assets. They are purchased with the idea that these assets will provide income in the future. Alternatively, the investor may choose to sell that asset later at a higher price for profit.[2]

So, just to recap, there are two ways you can grow your money through investing:

1. You earn an income (e.g. if you purchase shares, you may receive dividend payments).
2. You make a profit when you sell an asset because it has increased in value (hopefully its value won't have decreased, resulting in a loss).

## The importance of time

This is where the concept of time comes in, and it is really important. Time is what it is all about because an investment always involves an outlay today in the hope of a greater payoff in the future. In turn, this brings us to compound interest, a critical component of personal finances and investing – it is something worth keeping at the forefront of your mind.

Compound interest is essentially 'interest on interest'.[3] It is a method of calculating interest whereby that interest earned over time is then added to the amount invested before any returns. So, you can see why time is important here – the longer your money is invested, the more your money will grow and the more money you will end up with in the end.

This also obviously means that the earlier you start investing, the more wealth you can accumulate over time.

Here's an example:

When you invest, that first amount is called the 'principal'. Say you invest $1,000, this is your principal, and are set to earn a 5 per cent return. By the end of the year, you would gain an additional $50 and your balance would now stand at $1,050.

Assuming you reinvest you would now earn interest on $1,050. Each year you earn interest on the original principal plus interest on the interest you earn. In other words, it is compounded. Over a number of years this can really add up so that by the end of 10 years you would have $1,628.90.

Albert Einstein loved the concept of compound interest and is said to have described it as 'the eighth wonder of the world'. You have probably heard it before, but he is reported to have said: 'He who understands it, earns it. He who doesn't, pays it.' I am pretty sure that SHE who understands it also earns it!

There is much more we could cover on compound interest, but we have other topics to turn our attention to. The key takeaway is that compound interest matters, and you should keep it in mind as you figure out your financial and investment strategy. Think of it like a car rolling down a hill – it picks up more speed as it goes down the hill, gathering more momentum the longer it is allowed to roll. Compound interest is also why banks issue loans and depositors keep money at banks – it grows the money invested exponentially over time and that's worth a lot!

Oh, and one final thing – the time element forces investors to think about the long term because it requires one to look beyond the here and now. Long-termism is relevant to discussions on sustainable investing because many of the issues and problems we seek to address are often long term in nature but also with regard to solutions. Keep this in mind as you continue through the chapters ahead.

## RIDING THE UPS AND DOWNS

Before we get carried away, we need to talk about the downsides too, because investing is not solely about reaping (potential) financial returns. When you read some of the investing magazines or investor blogs, you might be forgiven for believing that investing is an easy path to getting rich quick. It's not. Sure, there are rewards involved, but investing also involves a whole heap of risks, possibly resulting in the worst outcome – losing all your money.

When we talk about saving, this doesn't involve a lot of risk as your money sits in a bank account. It earns steady interest, but this means it also doesn't involve a big financial return. However, when you move your capital into investing, you will probably be looking at taking more risk with your money and – hopefully but not inevitably – reaping bigger financial returns.

## What is risk, really?
In the world of all things finance, risk refers to the degree of uncertainty and/or the potential financial loss that may come along with an investment decision. As a general point, the bigger the risks you take as an investor, the higher the returns you will expect in order to be compensated for those risks.

As an investor, it is down to you to decide how much risk you want to accept. The good news is that there are many different levels of risk associated with how and where you invest, so you can actively determine what you are willing to accept. The important thing is to be aware of what you are doing. While you can't predict certain outcomes, you can be as informed as possible. This stands for investing in general, but also has some unique considerations as you move along the path of sustainable investing and seeking non-financial outcomes.

## WHAT ELSE DO I NEED TO KNOW?

### Portfolio diversification

Knowing how and where to start as an investor can be tough, but you have to start somewhere, the idea being that you eventually build towards having an investment plan or a strategy. Think about renovating your house; before you get started, you have a vision of what it will be like when it's finished. The same goes for your investment portfolio. You want to set your goals and then have a plan in place on how to reach them.

This is where portfolio diversification comes into your investment thinking. Simply put, diversification implies 'don't put all your eggs into one basket'. The goal of portfolio diversification is to apply this thinking to your investments and reduce the risk within your investment portfolio. The rationale behind this is that a portfolio constructed of different kinds of investments will, on average, yield higher returns and pose a lower risk than any individual investment within the portfolio.

Diversification comes along with many proven benefits. However, it does not guarantee an investor protection against a loss. It is also important to bear in mind that diversification does not reduce the systematic risk of investing in a particular market. This systematic risk is what is referred to as 'non-diversifiable risk' or 'market risk' – it is not associated with a particular company or industry, and will include inflation rate risk, exchange rate risk, political instability risk and interest rate risk. The factors outside a company's control that could impact on its performance.

There are many ways to diversify your investment portfolio – because diversification is, at its simplest, a strategy that ensures that the investor owns multiple types of investment assets. This means you can invest in a range of different assets classes, but you can also diversify within an asset class in order to improve the risk/return profile of your portfolio.

## What are asset classes and asset allocation?

Asset classes are essentially categories or neat ways to group investments or financial instruments – in particular, those that exhibit similar characteristics and are subject to the same laws and regulations.

The traditional definition includes three core asset classes:

- Stocks or public equities (also including exchange-traded funds (ETFs), a basket of securities that trade on an exchange, just like a stock)

- Fixed income or bonds

- Money market or cash equivalents

But there are other ways to invest – and these are often grouped into what is labelled 'alternative investments', such as:

- Venture capital and private equity

- Real estate (property)
- Commodities
- Foreign currency
- Collectibles

If you are looking for portfolio diversification, then you will look at your asset allocation. This is essentially how you divide your resources across the different investment categories (or asset classes) available to you. The idea is that an investor can lessen her risk because each asset class has a different relationship or correlation to the others.

## UNDERSTANDING THE DIFFERENT ASSET CLASSES

There's some argument about how many different types of asset class there are, but this book is not really the place for that discussion. Rather, let's run through the main asset classes that are commonly used and their different investment characteristics, so you are well versed to understand how these can be applied to the sustainable investing universe.

In this chapter we will cover the following categories because, as you will read in subsequent chapters, these asset classes or categories present the most exciting areas when looking at investment options through the sustainable investing lens:

- Stocks (also known as public equities)

- Exchange-traded funds (while not an asset class per se, this is in a section of its own because of the traction ETFs are getting with investors)

- Bonds (also known as fixed income)

- Private equity (one of the alternative asset classes we will cover because it's an interesting space for sustainable investors)

- Crowdfunding (not really considered an asset class in its own right, but there's some really cool stuff going on in crowdfunding)

- Angel investing (as with crowdfunding, it is not really an asset class, but it is something to be aware of if you want to get active in the investing world)

## STOCKS (ALSO KNOWN AS PUBLIC EQUITIES)

### What are stocks?

In a nutshell, stocks are an equity investment that represents ownership in a company. This entitles the holder of a company's equity to part of its earnings and assets. These stocks are called public equities when they are bought and sold through a public market such as the New York Stock Exchange, the Hong Kong Stock Exchange or the London Stock Exchange.

Bear in mind, there are different types of stock – with companies often offering the investor the right to buy either 'common' or 'preferred' stock. What is the difference?

- Common stock gives shareholders voting rights but no guarantee of dividend payments (payments made by the company to its shareholders usually as a distribution of profits). As the name suggests, this is the most common type of stock issued by companies. Most people who invest in public equities buy common stock.

- Preferred stock doesn't provide voting rights but usually guarantees a dividend payment. As a dividend is a distribution of a portion of the company's earnings, dividends are decided and allocated by the company's board of directors, usually requiring shareholders' approval. They can be paid monthly, quarterly, biannually or yearly.

## Why do investors like public equities?

There are a whole host of reasons why investors like to invest in the public equity market. Here are the main ones:

- **Investment gains.** One of the primary benefits of investing in public equity is the opportunity to potentially grow your money and to reap investment gains. Over time, the stock market tends to rise in value, though the prices of individual stocks will rise and fall daily. For example, let's look at the average annual return of a stock market index such as the S&P 500. This is a market-capitalisation-weight index of the 500 largest US publicly traded companies. The average annual return for the S&P 500 since its inception in

1928 through to 2018 is approximately 10 per cent[4] – although bear in mind that this 10 per cent average return when adjusted for inflation is around 7 per cent.

- **Dividend income.** As we've highlighted, some stocks may provide an income in the form of a dividend. These are additional payments made by the company, regardless of whether the stock has lost value on the stock market. These dividend payments represent an income to the investor that is on top of any gains from eventually selling the stock.

- **Liquidity.** Compared with many other asset classes, public equities are a relatively liquid asset. Liquidity, specifically financial liquidity, refers to how easily assets can be converted into cash. From an investor's perspective, a major advantage for public equity is its liquidity as most publicly traded stocks are available for purchase and easily traded. If trading on the main stock markets, the investor can usually buy and sell stock within seconds.

### What are the main risks with a public equity investment?

Investing in public equities through the stock market is a risky business because the price of stocks goes up and down, and this can be for many complex reasons. However, if you know the risks, you are better placed to mitigate them. There are many risks to consider, including:

- **Market risk (or systematic risk).** This is the risk of financial loss due to factors that affect an entire market or asset class. For example, economic recession or a stock market collapse will really hammer the price of most stocks. Take the global financial crisis of 2007/08 – during this bear market,[5] the S&P 500 lost 56 per cent of its value.[6] Some market risks that can affect stocks are not possible to prevent or foresee. Natural disasters (hurricanes, earthquakes, etc.) along with other events, like the COVID-19 pandemic, terrorist attacks, political instability or trade wars, can have major impacts on the value of stock investments.

- **Business risk (or unsystematic risk).** This risk relates to the financial loss associated with a specific company you may be invested in. It reflects certain factors that could lower the company's profit or lead to another type of failure by the company. For example, the stock value of a company may fall if it reports lower than expected earnings – any factor that threatens a company's ability to meet its targets, whether these be financial or performance-related. A recent example is Volkswagen during the diesel emissions scandal in 2015. After the news broke, the stock lost more than 30 per cent – virtually overnight.

- **Liquidity risk.** While stock markets are generally perceived as relatively liquid markets, liquidity can vary widely for individual companies and markets. Usually, smaller stock exchanges and lesser-known companies can be more difficult to sell, and the negative price impact can be substantial. This is something to be aware of in the public equities market – not all stocks can be bought and sold as easily as others.

## What is the difference between a growth stock and a value stock?

It is worth highlighting a couple of other definitions you should be aware of if you are considering moving into public equities – the difference between growth stocks and value stocks.

As the name implies, growth stocks are companies that have substantial potential for growth (defined either by revenues or cash flows, and definitely by profits) in the foreseeable future. Their main focus is to grow and, in order to achieve this, the company must devote current revenue toward further expansion. It makes sense, then, that these types of stocks don't often deliver dividends. Often growth stocks are younger companies with innovative products, but they can also be established companies with continuous high demand for their products. Growth stocks can provide substantial returns on capital but are often viewed as riskier and more volatile.

In contrast, value stocks are about finding diamonds in the rough – companies whose stock price doesn't fully reflect their fundamental worth. But bear in mind, the definition of what is good value is subjective and it takes a lot of time, experience and knowledge to identify undervalued companies. Value stocks are usually larger, more established companies that pay dividends and therefore may be considered less risky than growth stocks.

## How do you get into publicly listed stocks?

There are different ways to invest in the stock market.

Here are the most common:

- **Single stocks.** It is fairly easy to invest in single stocks and it doesn't take a fortune to get a well-diversified portfolio. However, it takes a lot of time and knowledge to find the right companies to invest in (particularly if you are a sustainable investor). Remember, it's not enough to find a business you believe in, you have to get in at the right price. If everyone already thinks it is a great business, it's probably already in a price range where there won't be much upside left.

- **Mutual equity fund.** If you feel you don't have the time and knowledge to invest in single stocks, you can choose to invest in a managed fund where a fund manager will do the job for you. With so many managed funds out there how do you find the right one? This is a good discussion to have with your financial advisor.

- **Equity exchange-traded funds.** Today there is a wide selection of equity ETFs. From ETFs with global equity market exposure, down to very specific themes, it's all there! ETFs have become an increasingly attractive investment opportunity for all types of investors so let's look at these in more detail.

## EXCHANGE-TRADED FUNDS

### What are ETFs?
An ETF, or exchange-traded fund, is basically a type of fund that 'owns' certain assets – these assets may include

stocks, bonds, commodities (a raw material that can be bought or sold) or futures (contracts for assets that are bought at an agreed price but are delivered and paid for at a later date). The ownership of the fund is then divided into shares that are traded on stock exchanges.

As with any tradable shares, investors can buy and sell ETFs via stock exchanges during trading hours. Like a stock, each ETF has a ticker symbol and a price that changes in real-time.

## Why do investors like ETFs?

ETFs provide many investors with an inexpensive, transparent and convenient way to get access to many different asset classes. You can see why they are popular:

- **Diversification.** So, we know that spreading your risk is a good thing and, compared to investing in single stocks, an ETF can give you exposure to a group of stocks, market segments or styles. You can also get ETFs in other asset classes and this can be a good thing for ensuring diversity across your portfolio.[7]

- **Lower fees.** One of the big reasons for the boom in ETFs is the lower cost incurred by the investor. While mutual funds can also give you diversification, ETFs are not actively managed (by an asset manager) and therefore they usually come at a lower cost. This is a big deal.

- **Easily traded.** You can buy an ETF like a stock, making it easily tradeable on an exchange, and at a price that is updated throughout the day. This makes them pretty liquid and attractive to many investors.

## What are the main risks with ETFs?

ETFs sound great, but before you rush in, take some time to fully consider some of the risks that can arise:

- **Trading risk.** Because ETFs are easily tradable, they are also exposed to trading risks associated with the price of buying and selling. And if you become an active trader, trading on a regular basis, costs will add up and eliminate the low fee benefit of ETFs. It's also worth bearing in mind that once you get into this mindset, you move away from being a long-term investor.

- **Liquidity risk.** Due to the fact that ETFs trade on a stock exchange, the level of liquidity in different ETFs can vary widely. An ETF has two prices, an 'ask' price – what you will pay for the shares – and a 'bid' price – the price at which you can sell the shares. The difference between the price of buying and selling is known as the 'spread'. Not all ETFs have a high trading volume (e.g. thinly traded ETFs – those that cannot be easily sold or exchanged for cash without a significant change in price), so you could find yourself in a situation where there is a large bid–ask spread. It's basically a pricing inefficiency that could cost you money if you can't get out of the investment when you want to.

- **Potential tracking error.** The difference between the returns of the index fund and the target index is known as a fund's 'tracking error'. When investing in an ETF you want the tracking error to be as low as possible. But this is not as easy as it might sound – and many ETFs can stray away from their intended index.

### How do you get into ETFs?

If you are thinking about including ETFs in your investment portfolio, it may be worth looking at some of the bigger ETF providers to understand the type of products and strategies in the market. This will help you understand more about what they are and what they do. Some of the biggest ETFs by asset size include the following (a good place to start would be to spend some time researching them online):

- BlackRock's iShares ETFs

- Vanguard ETFs

- State Street Global Advisors' SPDR ETFs

- Invesco PowerShares ETFs

## BONDS (ALSO KNOWN AS FIXED INCOME)

### What is a bond?

In brief, bonds are really just a form of loan where you (the investor) essentially serve as the 'bank'. The loan can be made to a wide range of recipients, be it a company, a city or a government, and the recipients are called 'the issuer'. In return for lending your money you receive regular interest payments, with the issuer agreeing to pay you back the face value of the loan on a specific date. There's quite a lot of certainty with bonds.

### Why do investors like bonds?

Unlike stocks, bonds don't give you any ownership rights. However, bonds are often viewed by many as a safer investment due to the steady stream of income they generate. So, when stock markets become volatile, investors often turn to bonds.

And if the bonds are held to maturity then the bondholder will receive the entire principal (loan) back – this makes them a pretty smart way to preserve your capital while investing.

### What are the main risks with bonds?

While providing a predictable income stream, bonds are not risk-free for the investor. There are many potential risks to consider when thinking about investing in bonds. Here are some of the main ones:

- **Interest rate risk.** This is probably the best-known risk when it comes to bonds investing. When interest rates fall, bond prices tend to rise. And when interest rates rise, bond prices tend to fall. This obviously means that you (the investor) have some exposure to changes in the interest rate. Put it another way, when buying the bond you are committed to receiving a fixed rate of return (the interest payments you will receive on the 'loan') – if the market interest rate goes up after you have bought it, the bond will then trade at a discount. This inverse relationship is to do with the supply and demand for the bond in a changing interest rate environment and reflects the lower return the investor will make on the bond.

- **Credit quality.** When investing in bonds, you also have to take into account the credit quality of the issuer – the risk being that the issuer is unable to pay the interest, or the principal as contractually defined – and doing so is not always straightforward. Some bonds are issued from governments – most federal governments have very high credit ratings and are generally considered pretty safe. Some bonds are issued by companies and this will depend on the credit rating of the company. A bond from the US government (known as Treasuries) is considered much safer than a bond from a small emerging company with a low credit rating.

- **Loan duration.** How long you lend the money to the issuer also has an impact on risk. Bonds with longer durations are paid more – why? Because it means your money is tied up for a longer period and you are more exposed to inflation risks; when the rate of price increases in the economy, it essentially brings down the returns paid out by the bond.

## How do you get into bonds?

As with all asset classes, there are different ways to invest in the bond market. Here are the three most common investment options:

- **Single bonds.** An investor can buy single bonds. However, you need to have a good chunk of money to get a well-diversified portfolio if you are going to go into single bonds. You will probably also need to spend a great amount of time assessing the quality of the issuers for the reasons mentioned above.

- **Bond mutual funds.** A more common way for private investors to access the bond markets is to buy a bond mutual fund. A bond fund does not have a set maturity date, as it continuously invests in bonds with different maturity dates. This provides the investor with exposure to different investments and time periods and can help with diversification.

- **Bond ETFs.** Basically, a type of exchange-traded fund that exclusively invests in bonds. These are similar to bond mutual funds, because they hold a bunch of bonds with different strategies (e.g. holding periods, issuers, etc.).

## PRIVATE EQUITY

### What is private equity?
Private equity (PE) refers to investment in private companies that have not 'gone public' (in other words, companies that have not listed on a public stock exchange). In their simplest form, private equity firms comprise investors who want to invest directly in companies, rather than buying company stock – pooling money into private equity 'funds'.

So how does this work? PE firms raise capital from different sources, such as pension funds, insurance companies, endowments and high-net-worth individuals. These investors band together as Limited Partners (LPs) with a fund manager – known as the General Partner (GP) – who is responsible for leading and managing the fund. Often taking a majority stake in the companies they invest in (known as the investee), the PE firm aims to improve the operational performance of these companies by increasing growth and/or cutting costs. The idea is then to sell the investee company for a profit at a later date.

Because these funds are structured as long-term investment vehicles, LPs are often required to commit their capital for the fund's total life – typically 10 years. A fund's life cycle is usually broken down into an initial five-year investment period followed by a five-year divestment period.

## So how does a private equity firm generate returns for the investors?

Private equity and venture capital funds generate returns by selling their stake in a business for a higher price than they initially acquired it for, thereby creating a capital gain. This process is called an 'exit' and is achieved through selling the stake in the company, possibly through one of the following:

- An initial public offering (IPO)

- Selling to a strategic buyer (a trade sale)

- Selling to another PE firm (a secondary buyout)
- Selling to the company's management (buy-back)

Generally, the exit takes place somewhere between three and seven years after the original investment, representing long-term ownership during which significant operational and other changes can be made. This is an interesting dynamic for a sustainable investor who might be looking to the long term as well.

## Why do investors like private equity?

Private equity investors are usually looking to improve the risk and reward characteristics of their investment portfolio. Because investing in private equity can offer the opportunity to generate higher absolute returns while improving portfolio diversification, it's a popular asset class with many investors. Reasons include:

- **Long-term historical out-performance.** The long-term returns of private equity can represent a premium to the performance of public equities – in other words, deliver higher returns to the investor.[8]

- **True stock picking.** Since private equity funds own large (and often controlling) stakes in companies, few other private equity managers will have access to the same companies. PE managers therefore can be true 'stock pickers'. This contrasts with mutual funds, which often hold pretty much the same underlying investments as their peer group, with variations in weightings being fine-tuned to a few basis points (a basis point is one hundredth of a percentage point and usually used to express changes in interest rates).

- **Portfolio diversification.** Within a balanced portfolio, the introduction of private equity can improve diversification.

## What are the main risks with a private equity investment?

Investing in private equity is very different from investing in the public markets. And it's a risky business because, if the investee company stumbles, the PE fund and its investors will lose money. As with all investments, it is very important to know where the potential risks lie. Here are just a few to consider:

- **Liquidity risk.** Private equity investments cannot be easily bought and sold on a secondary market, making them less liquid (in other words, harder to get out with cash). A PE investor needs a long-time horizon, at least five to ten years.

- **Transparency risk.** Private companies are not required to be as transparent as public companies, being exempt from issuing a prospectus and often being able to choose which information to make public. This makes the investor's job more challenging and often means a lot of trust must be put in the investment manager to do a good job.

- **High cost.** The fees for an investment in a PE fund are usually very high. A typical fee structure for a PE investment is often called the '2 & 20' – a 2 per cent annual fee on an investment, plus a 20 per cent share of profits at the fund's end date.

- **Positive skewness.** The median return of private equity is much lower than the mean (arithmetic average) return. The relatively high average return reflects the small possibility of a truly outstanding return, combined with the much larger probability of a more modest or negative return. Worth bearing in mind!

## What is the difference between private equity and venture capital?

You may well have heard the terms 'private equity' and 'venture capital' in the same breath. But there is a difference. Private equity investors are all about improving a current business in order to make the company (more) profitable. They typically buy out the business in its entirety, in order to have the freedom to restructure it and change things around. PE firms will then do everything in their power to turn the business around, often bringing in new management and changing methods to become more profitable.

Venture capital is different. VC investors are about finding good deals in young businesses and new companies. Venture capitalists may own a portion of a business but, in contrast to PE firms, they rarely buy a company outright. They offer to invest a set amount of money for a stake in the company. Venture capitalists may want a say in how the company is run or alternatively may be very hands-off.

## So how do you get into private equity?

It's not that easy. As an individual investor it is a tough asset class to get into – historically reserved for large pension funds and university endowments. Typically, only the wealthiest can afford the large sums demanded for direct access to private equity funds run by famous names such as Blackstone, Apollo and Carlyle. Many funds may require a minimum investment of $1 million, $5 million or more. Also do remember, this minimum investment is compounded by high fees.

But equity crowdfunding is changing the PE landscape, allowing anyone to invest in non-public companies. Equity crowdfunding enables broad groups of investors to come together via an online platform to fund start-up companies and small businesses in return for equity. Investors invest their money in a business and receive ownership of a small piece of that business. If the business succeeds, then its value goes up, as well as the value of a share in that business – but of course, the converse is also true. More below.

## CROWDFUNDING

## What is crowdfunding?

The crowdfunding phenomenon has only gone truly mainstream in the last few years. But the concept itself is certainly not new. One of the first crowd funds actually dates back to the late 19th century – for the base of the Statue of

Liberty (the statue itself was a gift from the French). To fund the $300,000 needed for the pedestal, citizens were invited to donate – even small amounts – enticed by miniature replicas of the statue given in return. Love that!

Crowdfunding involves raising many small amounts of money from a large number of people, typically via an online platform. While the concept is simple, there are in fact different designs:

- **Reward-based:** usually list products, services, projects or simply an idea, allowing the backer to pledge an amount of money for a 'reward' – and structured such that the largest backers receive the highest value or a unique reward. Some of the first and best-known reward-based platforms are Kickstarter and Crowdfunder.

- **Equity-funding:** enables start-ups, early- and growth-stage businesses to raise finance from a 'crowd' of everyday investors, professionals, angels (individuals seeking to invest in start-ups) and venture capital firms, in return for an equity stake in the business. Investments can be small, starting from double digit $-amounts. In return for their investments, the investors get a pro-rata equity stake in the business. Some of the major platforms include Indiegogo and CircleUp.

- **Peer-to-peer lending:** often seen as a direct alternative to a bank loan, the difference being that, instead of borrowing from a single source, companies and private individuals can borrow directly from tens or hundreds of individuals who are ready to lend. The idea is to cut out the middle person so that both parties get a better deal. Some well-known peer-to-peer lending platforms include Zopa and Funding Societies.

- **Donation-based:** backers donating varying sums of money to support a specific cause or project. Sometimes they will receive a simple 'thank you' or a special mention – or even a physical item such as a postcard. The pledge is pretty much a donation. Platforms include Causes, Chuffed and Classy.

## Why do investors like crowdfunding?

There are a whole host of reasons why investors like crowdfunding:

- **Accessible and democratic.** Crowdfunding is a really innovative way to provide all investors, large and small, with opportunities to invest their money in companies that appeal to them. This makes crowdfunding a pretty democratic way to bring investing to the masses. Platforms are online and easy to access – to create an account and start investing can take a matter of minutes. And you don't need a fat wallet to get started – investments can start from small amounts, making it a very inclusive asset class.

- **Supports innovation.** As a crowdfunding investor, it is possible to discover exciting innovations in tech and design before they go mainstream. Many companies on crowdfunding platforms are in the early product development phase, with products that have not yet been officially launched.

- **Potentially higher returns.** With equity crowdfunding, one of the big attractions for many investors is the opportunity to make higher returns than those offered by other assets such as bonds or publicly listed equities. The risks are often higher, as you will likely be investing in start-ups, but few other investment opportunities offer the potential to increase wealth as much as equity in an early-stage business.

- **Diversification.** Since initial investments can be quite small it is possible to get a well-diversified portfolio without a huge investment. Given that the risk profile of many firms seeking crowdfunding differs from the traditional equity market, it can allow investors to spread their risk and make sure portfolios are diversified, through investing in a number of companies.

- **Rewards.** Many companies offer 'rewards' as part of their pitch. Investors can be one of the first to try new products or get other benefits such as discounts or vouchers.

## What are the main risks with crowdfunding?

As with any investment, there are risks associated with crowdfunding investments, particularly as crowdfunding also includes the various risks that go hand in hand when investing in start-ups:

- **Business failure.** As many of the companies listed on the crowdfunding platforms are at the early stage, there is a high risk that the business will not take off as planned. This might lead to lower than expected returns or even a total loss of the investment if a company goes bust. This is why diversification is important, spreading risk across many small investments instead of a few big bets.

- **Illiquid investment.** Even if the business is doing well, it might take a long time for you to get your money back. It's still fairly difficult to trade these types of investments so options are limited if you want to get your money out – investors should expect money to be invested for the long term.

- **Dilution risk.** If the business raises more funds at a later date (which most start-ups do), the percentage of equity you hold in it may decrease relative to what you originally bought.

### So how do you get into crowdfunding?

The good news is that it is fairly easy to get started with crowdfund investing: the market is really about getting private individuals on board. As an investor you have to decide what kind of crowdfunding platform or approach you are interested in. And then simply get started!

## ANGEL INVESTING

### What is angel investing?

Angel investing is basically all about individual investors providing capital to start-up or early-stage businesses.

The angel investor gives financial backing to small start-ups, usually in exchange for some ownership equity in the company. An angel investor may also be known as a private investor, seed investor or angel funder. Quite often, you will find angel investors among the entrepreneur's family and friends network.

I raise angel investing here because it is emerging as an exciting platform for investors who want to get into the 'weeds' of early-stage companies – and it has a great deal of relevance to us sustainable investors, because of the investment opportunities that arise and the ability to pick and choose according to your values.

## Why do investors like angel investing?

People who get into angel investing tend to do so for a number of reasons. These may include:

- **Potential for a solid return.** While a risky form of investing, the flip side is that angel investors may stand to make good financial returns. Your typical angel investor is probably hoping that they will receive a higher return on their investment than they can get on the stock market.

- **Altruism (or hedonism?).** Many angel investors are successful entrepreneurs themselves and reap personal benefits from helping to build a thriving and successful company. They may enjoy helping their local community or developing a new environmental technology. Of course, there are also your hedonistic angels who thrive on the thrill of creating something new!

- **Opportunity to be involved.** Many angel investors invest not just their money, but also their time, seeking the opportunity to be involved and to participate in building the company. Some want to act as a mentor, while others look to have a seat on the company's board.

## What are the main risks with angel investing?

Angel investing is risky because you are investing in early-stage companies that have a long way to go before having viable and durable business and revenue models.

- **Business failure.** As with crowdfunding, if you are investing in companies that are yet to take off, there is a high risk that they will never do so. The majority of start-ups fail within the first few years – only about 10 per cent of start-ups will exist after the five-year mark – so the risk of the total loss of your investment is pretty high.[9]

- **Illiquid investment.** Because an angel is buying private stock, it cannot be publicly traded and this makes it quite an illiquid investment. If you need to get out, you may be unable to.

- **Ownership dilution.** If the company you invest in as an angel becomes successful, it is likely to attract new investors. This is usually a good thing but be wary of what it can mean for your ownership amount. If you haven't drawn up a contract that protects you as an angel, you may end up very diluted in terms of your ownership.

## So how do you get into angel investing?

There are a few avenues to explore:

1. As a direct investor. You will be investing directly in a company so it can be hands-on, but it can also be very time-consuming.
2. Through intermediaries such as an investment fund. This is a good way to learn from others who may have more experience with angel investing as well as diversifying your risk because you will be investing in several companies.
3. Joining an angel investment group. When angels form a group, they can benefit from their combined business perspectives and experiences. Before joining a group, do your due diligence to check if the investors involved are aligned with your thinking.

## WHAT IS THE PURPOSE OF CAPITAL?

Now we have been through the nuts and bolts, I hope you will feel more comfortable talking about what investing actually is, and how it can be done. The critical thing to remember is that investing is not saving. Investing is about using your wealth to put it into an asset in the hope of a greater payoff in the future.

With that in mind, let's return to the more philosophical questions we posited at the outset of the chapter:

- What is the real purpose of capital?[10] Of wealth?

- What do we look for when we commit financial wealth to certain projects or businesses?

- What role does the corporate world play in our economies and societies?

- Should a company have a social conscience and, if so, societal responsibilities?

- How can we define what these responsibilities might be?

This is where we introduce the link between how we invest (where we deploy our money) and the type of world we want to build (in particular, the kind of companies and sectors we want to invest our capital in). Perhaps you have considered this at length, or perhaps you haven't thought about it all. Based on the conversations I've had with many diverse people over the years, I can see that we are still struggling to see these linkages. I would also contend that it is partly to do with how the financial industry has kept the ordinary woman (and man) at bay – with confusing language, high fees and generally exclusionary behaviour.

Until we really think through this question, at a deep and emotional level, we will continue to see investing simply as finance. But at some point, as we stand in a world on the brink of environmental crisis, and with social and economic inequalities increasing, we have to ask ourselves if we are getting it wrong.

We've touched on the risk and return components of investing. These have always been defined as financial risk and financial return. But is this the right way to look at things? If we want to explore how we create value, value for ourselves but also our world, we should consider value not simply through a financial lens but also thinking about broader (and more powerful) non-financial values and impact.

Ultimately, this brings us to question the system as a whole – and really much of the investment and finance world has been built around capitalism and the workings that sit around the capital model. We are beginning to hear quiet murmurings from all corners about whether we should be stripping back how we define capitalism and the benefits it has promised, and in many circumstances failed, to deliver.

## FINAL THOUGHTS BEFORE YOU READ ON...

There's a great deal more to the investing game so I urge you to take some time out to learn more about the basics – 'investing 101' if you like. What is covered in this chapter is simply enough to help you with the rest of the book, but it's by no means the launch pad to start actively investing. This shouldn't be done until you have chatted to a few investment professionals, enquired with your bank and sought out what friends and family members might be doing on the investment front.

As you do this, here are a few tips:

- Do learn about investing yourself – part of what will close the investment gap is women getting stuck in and taking action themselves.

- Be clear on your goals – decide what is important to you and don't be told what your goal should be.

- Figure out how you feel about risk – this is really understanding what kind of growth you are looking for, and the level of risk you are OK with taking on, to potentially achieve that growth.

- Talk to others – whether this be a friend or a financial planner. It's always useful to bounce ideas off someone else.

- It's an ongoing process – so keep learning, keep practising, keep listening.

# FOUR

# WHEN 'SUSTAINABLE INVESTING' BECOMES JUST 'INVESTING'

By this point, it is likely you have a strong sense of where this book is heading. The concept of wealth, and the narrative that sits around it, is indeed changing. And we, as women, can and will play a significant role in making this change happen. Wealth, however big or small, is a privilege and for this reason it comes with certain responsibilities, particularly in a world where resources are increasingly constrained and inequality gaps are rapidly widening.

The scope of this chapter is to help you start dipping your toes in the sustainable investing waters. The desired outcome is that you will feel comfortable with the terms and concepts that you may encounter. The goal is to provide you with enough information to hold your own in a conversation with a financial advisor, or someone from your bank, or a friend who is keen to learn more.

As with many things financial, there is a lot of terminology and lingo thrown around, sometimes resulting in confusion and potentially off-putting. But please don't let it! This is about deciphering the field and setting you up to feel confident in the actions you can take.

At some point, you will move into the hows and the whats, including different frameworks and tools that can help you think through your own personal plan of attack. For now, let's focus on what sustainable investing means – in the broader sense – and how this relates to the world around us. This has to include some discussion on concrete definitions because it's still quite muddy, with different people using different terms for what essentially can be the same thing. Or at the very least, they are talking about a similar vehicle that is moving in the same direction.

This chapter will also provide you with a potted history of sustainable investing and a sense of where it is headed, particularly in terms of who is doing what and the growth we are starting to see. We also bust a few myths that might be playing on your mind – there are some people in the financial industry who have done quite a good job at promoting these myths, so it is worth taking the time to look at the facts.

## WHAT'S IN A NAME?

Thus far, the term 'sustainable investing' has been bandied about in this book as though we all agree on what we are talking about. There are in fact a number of differently nuanced interpretations of what sustainable investing means, as well as competing terms. To be honest, definitions have been subject to a great deal of debate for a number of years, often reflecting a person's professional background, specific industry or specific regional context.

That said, don't get too hung up on having a neat, capsule-sized definition. For us individual investors, as you will learn, sustainable investing is a somewhat more personal reflection of your values and priorities. In our context and at this point in time, I honestly think it's good enough to say 'I am trying to achieve something more than just making more money with my investments'.

On a positive note, it is also worth pointing out that, in the last couple of years, the financial industry has come together much more and committed to clearer working definitions. For the purpose of this book, and for the purpose of building a movement that engages with women and shows them how they can use their wealth, I do believe it is important to put a stake in the ground, by which we can measure how far we move in the future.

## LABELLING SUSTAINABLE INVESTING

If you have been thinking about sustainable investing for some time, it's quite likely that you have heard of a number of different terms that seem somewhat related. These may include:

- sustainable and responsible investment

- impact investing

- socially responsible investing

- ESG investing

- ethical investing

Each of these terms represents slightly varied backgrounds or approaches, but there is a commonality – the goal of achieving positive change in an area or on an issue which the investor is passionate about, and these areas invariably have a social and/or environmental dimension.

Here is a formal definition that works well, from the US Sustainable Investment Forum (US SIF).[1] I like this because it is all-encompassing and reflects different traditions and ambitions:

> Sustainable, responsible and impact investing (SRI) is an investment discipline that considers environmental, social and corporate governance (ESG) criteria to generate long-term competitive financial returns and positive societal impact.

As you will have gathered by now, I am using the label 'sustainable investing'. I only mention other labels so that you are aware of them and that sustainable investing is umbrella-like in nature. I also think there is something smart about using the term 'sustainable investing' – because when you look at companies that are both socially and environmentally responsible, it makes sense that these will perform better in the long run, right? It makes sense that these companies would be described as sustainable.

This is because these companies are getting to grips with real and pressing business risks – such as water scarcity, the impact of climate change or improving the labour rights of the people they employ or who work in their supply chain. It makes sense that these risks will directly or indirectly impact on these companies (and the companies' share prices) in the future. So, using the word 'sustainable' implies that we, as investors, are looking to the long-term health and performance of the companies we invest in.

## BREAKING IT DOWN – GIVE US AN E, GIVE US AN S, GIVE US A G

OK, so having said we shouldn't get too hung up on definitions, it is, however, important to understand that there are different components that comprise sustainable investing. In particular, in the financial industry, people now talk about 'ESG' – Environmental, Social and Governance – investing (as you will have noted in the list above!).

Many institutional investors, asset and wealth managers now have sustainable investment professionals who commit substantial time and energy to building ESG frameworks, policies and processes. And it's a reflection of the times that ESG is now an industry buzzword and you don't have to spell out what it means. These investment teams use ESG factors or criteria to understand what could affect a company's profits, opportunities and risks in the future. It is effectively a lens through which to understand the broader range of influences that can determine how well the company performs over the long term. This lens helps identify potential risks that could affect the performance of the company, as well as opportunities to create value for the company, investors and broader stakeholders in the world.

For you and me, ESG represents certain things when looking at a company that we may want to invest in:

- **E – the environment.** This is about looking at what impact a company has on the resources that sustain it, either directly or indirectly. This can be pretty broad. For example, it might include the contribution that the company makes to climate change, measured through factors such as greenhouse gas (GHG) emissions or potential climate solutions. Other environmental considerations could include energy efficiency, biodiversity impact or waste management efforts. Increasingly, investors are looking at what companies are specifically doing to decarbonise production processes, supply chains and final products because these can quite often represent tangible actions.

- **S – social factors.** This includes all issues that relate to the company's role in society, such as labour standards, how a company treats suppliers or interacts with the communities it operates in. Hot topics include any exposure to illegal child labour, but also more mundane matters to do with health and safety management. Relations with local communities are fundamental because this often determines whether or not a company has a 'social licence' to operate.

- **G – governance.** Governance is all about the rules or principles that determine the relationship between the management of a company and the various stakeholders in the company (such as employees, shareholders, workers' unions). So, we would look at things like transparency of decisions, directors' pay and internal controls. A company that has a well-defined corporate governance structure should be doing a good job of aligning its interests with other stakeholders. This can be a powerful tool for assessing its long-term success. I am also a big believer that if a company is well governed (i.e. it is doing the right thing on things like transparency, diversity, internal checks and balances), it is highly likely it will also be on top of other long-term risks such as climate change.

Getting to grips with these ESG components is important because it helps you categorise the kind of issues you will want to consider when looking at companies or funds. It is also likely that, when you move into action, you will hear different players talk about ESG. In particular, if you speak with a wealth manager or financial advisor, they may talk about the ESG strategy that they use, perhaps ESG screens that they apply.[2]

Those in the investment industry might do that in different ways such as applying ESG factors to complement their traditional financial analysis as a way to ensure that they are identifying companies with strong sustainability practices and hopefully reducing risk exposures. They might also have a due diligence process in place when they use other fund managers to make sure they are influencing positive change in the company or sector. Some investors also actively engage with the companies that they invest in. Often called corporate engagement and shareholder action, this refers to the measures an investor might employ to use their shareholder power to influence company behaviour – for example, privately engaging with the company's management on ESG issues that they believe to be critical to the business or perhaps filing a shareholder proposal, put to the vote at the company's annual general meeting.[3]

## A WORD ON IMPACT INVESTING

Impact investing is one term that you might have heard quite a bit about, and it can be somewhat confusing when you think about where it lies in relation to the bigger umbrella terms. Until recently, it was often described as a subset of sustainable investing. The term itself was first coined back in 2007, when the great and the good from the investment community gathered in the Rockefeller Foundation's Bellagio Center on Lake Como, Italy.[4]

In its simplest form, impact investments are those that aim to generate a financial return as well as a social benefit. You may have also heard of people talk about 'double bottom line investments' because investors are looking beyond financial return, to leverage capital to bring about some other kind of return – or impact.[5]

What does that mean in terms of ESG? Well, a purist would probably say that ESG investing is about looking at a company's ESG practices alongside the more traditional financial analysis that an investor would do. Impact investing, in contrast, looks at how a company (or even a non-profit organisation) delivers certain activities or projects that bring a positive benefit to society.

If you want to learn more about the specifics of this debate, take a look at the website of the GIIN (Global Impact Investing Network), which gives this definition:

> Impact investments are investments made with the intention to generate positive, measurable social and environmental impact alongside a financial return. Impact investments can be made in both emerging and developed markets and target a range of returns from below market to market rate, depending on investors' strategic goals.[6]

To a certain extent, I interpret this current definition as somewhat a convergence in thinking, with impact investing aligning with other definitions. To be honest, at times I do use terms interchangeably and you will see some of that reflected in this book – perhaps the telling difference being reference to below market returns which may have been something an impact investor was traditionally more comfortable with accepting. But there's more to come on the financial returns discussion, as this has been a thorn in the side for sustainable investment proponents.

## A POTTED HISTORY OF SUSTAINABLE INVESTING

Now that we are all on the same page with regard to definitions and the terms we will use, you may be wondering where this all came from. Or perhaps, like me, why it took so long to make it into a book targeting women like us. A brief history of how sustainable investing came about and has evolved over time, along with a vision of where it is heading, is definitely in order.

### Back in the day

It is probably fair to say that the roots of sustainable investing date back many hundreds of years. If you look at various religious influences, you can observe many teachings that align with some of the principles of sustainable investing we see today. For example, in biblical times, some observed that 'ethical investing' was required under Jewish law whereby ownership carries certain rights and responsibilities, and rules were set to correct societal imbalances.

At the same time, there are strong parallels with other faiths – such as the principles enshrined in Islamic finance, which are based on the sacred law of the religion requiring that Muslims must not conduct business involving forbidden items or activities. Born from the religious teachings of the Qur'an, this has been translated into certain forbidden investment activities under shariah law and extends to forbidding all interest payments.

Then moving into the 18th century, the money management practices of the Methodists were taking shape, encouraging followers to avoid investing in, or partnering with, anyone or anything which made a profit from gambling, alcohol, tobacco or weapons. In a way, this was the first form of 'social screening' – essentially applying screens on what is considered 'in' and what is 'out'.

## Social issues, the swinging sixties, divestment and beyond

It wasn't really until the 1960s that the concept of sustainable investing became formalised in any shape or form. Much of this arose from concern about social issues of the day – in particular, the impact of the civil rights movement.

In fact, the first real 'win' for sustainable investing was the role it played in ending apartheid in South Africa. As the fund management industry grew, active investors recognised that they could play a role in influencing corporate behaviour. By 'divesting' from South African companies (divesting being the process of selling an asset, in this case the investor getting out of their shareholding in a company) the international investment community became an impetus to force change and end apartheid. From the 1980s, when divestment began, to when the De Klerk administration took action to end apartheid in 1993, a whopping $625 billion in investments were directed away from South Africa.

Interestingly, student protestors also played an important role, demanding that universities cease investing in companies doing business with South Africa. This student voice and its success in pushing university endowments to take action on social and environmental issues is really significant. We also saw this in 2010, when the fossil fuel divestment campaign began to emerge on campuses in the United States. The movement has proliferated since, moving beyond the US to universities around the world. It is estimated that, by 2019, $11 trillion has been committed to divest out of fossil fuel companies.[7] People power is doing it again!

Environmental worries have of course been central in the development of sustainable investing. From the 1980s, events such as the Bhopal chemical gas disaster in 1984 and the Exxon Valdez oil spill in 1989 began to shine a light on the role of companies in safeguarding human life, protecting our environment and their responsibilities beyond turning a profit.

## Fast forward to the 2000s
In 2005, Kofi Annan, the then Secretary-General of the United Nations, invited a group of institutional investors to band together to draw up the 'Principles for Responsible

Investment' (PRI). These were then launched at the New York Stock Exchange in 2006.

What are these principles all about? The idea was to provide the financial industry with a voluntary set of principles which encourage and drive investors to build ESG into their thinking and decision-making. The end goal of the UN-supported PRI is to collectively build a sustainable global financial system, with long-term value creation at its heart. The PRI as an organisation argues that such a system will reward long-term, responsible investment and benefit the environment and society as a whole.

Watching the growth in the PRI has been phenomenal. By 2020, $90 trillion of assets under management (AUM) were signed up to the principles, representing a huge amount of the world's wealth.[8]

It is worth also pointing out that the 2008 global financial crisis was a bit of a wake-up call in terms of demonstrating how financial markets are so closely interlinked with our economies and our societies. For some, it was a stark reminder that pursuing market growth does not always result in benefits for all and that the greater good is often demoted in the pursuit of profit.

The global financial crisis focused attention on the role of investors and their responsibility as good stewards of capital. For any observer of the crash, it is hard to avoid questioning what the concept of stewardship means and why so many were failed in this regard. Post-crisis, a whole heap of financial regulation followed – and so too did the increased awareness among the public about the role of the financial industry in society. While we don't seem to have learned all the lessons we should have from the past, we have had a shift in perception and subsequent expectations of the industry.

## HOW BIG ARE WE TALKING? GROWTH IN THE SUSTAINABLE INVESTMENT MARKET

It's worth taking a moment to reflect on size – how big are we talking? As we've seen from the growth in signatories to the PRI, interest in ESG investment criteria has grown rapidly among the asset and wealth management community. While it hasn't gone from nothing to everything overnight, the financial industry has really started to move forward.

This has probably happened due to a timely combination of regulatory change (especially where financial market regulators have pushed for listed companies to disclose to the investors what they are up to on the ESG front) and customer demand (whereby both institutional and retail investors are now seeing that many of these issues are also ultimately financial issues). Now looking across the industry, it is probably fair to assume that the majority of investment portfolios will include at least one ESG fund and that ESG screenings are now being imposed on other funds.

## The big ones – the institutional investors

To get a sense of what this means, let's take a look at the institutional world specifically (i.e. large organisational investors who invest on behalf of their 'members'; this would include pension funds, insurance companies, endowment funds, mutual funds and commercial banks). For the last 20 years, some of the more innovative institutional investors, along with other forward-thinking, high-net-worth individuals and foundations, have been developing approaches, experimenting with instruments and building processes.

How big is big? There are a few numbers that float around and some dependency on how you define sustainable investing. If you are interested in understanding more, a good place to start would be the *Global Sustainable Investment Review 2018*, probably the most comprehensive study out there, gathering findings from market studies of the various regional sustainable investment forums, in Europe, the US, Canada, Japan and Australia.[9] It provides a good snapshot of what is happening in the institutional investment world. The most recent report found that sustainable investment had surged worldwide by more than a third since 2016, reaching assets of more than $30 trillion at the start of 2018.

What does this actually mean? Well, it is a tally of the professionally managed assets that use some kind of sustainable investment approach. Basically, considering ESG factors in the investment portfolio selection and management process. We explore these terms and definitions in Chapter 5, but for now, the point is to recognise that sustainable investing has become increasingly important to many in the industry and it is influencing the behaviour of those companies and others in the financial sector that seek their investments.

## Individual investors – the 'retail investment market'

In turn, this is now taking hold in the retail market with many individuals, particularly younger generations and women (as we already know), caring about what type of businesses they are investing in. Comprehensive data is harder to come by, but it is fair to say that retail assets are growing.

For example, according to the latest report from the European Sustainable Investment Forum (Eurosif), retail assets in Europe now account for more than 30 per cent of sustainable investments. This is compared to just 3.4 per cent in 2013. It is also expected that these investors will increase their allocation to sustainable investments from 38 per cent of their investment portfolio to 48 per cent within five years from the date of the report.[10] In the US, research by Morningstar found that 72 per cent of respondents expressed at least a moderate interest in sustainable investing.[11]

## Demand versus supply

As demand is growing, one of the challenges that we face is that demand is now outstripping supply. There are some concerns that there is a shortage of high-quality investment opportunities and we will talk about this later in the book. The good news is that the financial industry is recognising this challenge and working to bring more suitable investment products to market.

The ranks of sustainable funds have certainly continued to grow. By the end of 2019, Morningstar reported that, in the US, there were 564 'ESG consideration' funds with $933 billion in assets under management.[12] This climbed up from 351 in 2018. In another example of increasing supply, Blackrock has indicated that it plans to double the number of ESG ETFs it offers to 150 by 2021, as well as to begin offering sustainable versions of its model portfolios.[13]

Technology also has a role to play in solving this problem, with online platforms increasing access to sustainable investment opportunities, at the same time as overcoming geographical boundaries. Chapter 12 is dedicated to looking at just how technology holds an important key to unlocking the retail sustainable investment market.

## SO WHY DO IT? WHAT'S IN IT FOR YOU?

Let's assume you are already inspired and energised to become an active investor. You are galvanised to start investing your money – and let's face it, looking at some of the scary numbers in earlier chapters, as a woman, this should be a no-brainer. However, you may now be asking yourself – if I am going to invest, surely I should just be focusing on maximising financial returns? Or perhaps – I don't really have the time to learn more about sustainable investing so why bother? Or simply – why would I do this?

Of course, any investment strategy will have upsides and downsides. You have to determine what feels right for you and really understand why you are making a decision so you can move forward with confidence. To this end, it may be useful to spell out some of the pros and cons of sustainable investing that you may want to reflect on. It is a very personal decision so don't feel you have to rush it, nor that all of the following has to hold true for you.

## Look to the positive – some of the pros

- **Setting your own rules.** By taking a stand, you are investing based on your personal values. This means it is your call. Your investment portfolio becomes a reflection of who you are and the values you chose to live by. Quite literally, you will be putting your money where your mouth is, and you can't deny that there is something hugely empowering about that.

- **Leveraging your influence.** By being an active sustainable investor, you are using your leverage to influence the behaviour of companies, industries and sectors, and the financial markets. You don't have to be a bystander or a victim. You have multiple voices, money being one of them.

- **Furthering certain causes.** Your money, your wealth, goes to where you want it to go. By seeking out companies which operate according to certain standards or objectives (e.g. strong environmental behaviour, active diversity strategies, balanced and fair employee policies) you are directing your cash towards companies that further causes close to your heart. That finance can be a tool to address specific social and environmental challenges. And what's not to love about that?

- **Driving long-term outperformance.** By considering the social and environmental exposures you have in your investments, you are probably also looking out for the long term. A growing body of evidence shows us that companies with robust sustainability approaches and performance tend to financially outperform comparable companies with bad sustainability records. Think about fossil fuel companies (admittedly, this is a tricky and often emotive sector to consider). At the moment, a number of fossil fuel companies are still some of the most profitable in the world. Why? Largely because we are not pricing in the massive externalities (the cost or the benefit of an activity to an unrelated third party) that these companies produce (carbon emissions, air pollution) and the sector continues to receive huge government subsidies. But if you look at where we stand in terms of climate change and the required response, these companies cannot continue on this trajectory. From the investor perspective, being aware of what global climate commitments will mean for the sector will also force you to consider what companies will be successful in the long term.

## Keep a balanced perspective – some of the cons

- **Making careful decisions.** Aligning your investment decisions with your values is fantastic (obviously I am biased). But don't go overboard in terms of following passions and ideals over smart decisions. If you are too rigid in your beliefs, you may exclude potential funds and companies that are actually pretty good in terms of sustainable investing options. This is where working with an investment professional (someone who can fully explore with you what you want to achieve with your investments) can really help keep you on track.

- **Being aware of greenwashing.** Some companies and funds can do a good job at greenwashing (or any other kind of 'washing'). Corporate marketing and PR efforts can hide a whole host of sins and this makes our job as sustainable investors even harder. Do your best research, check against third-party sources and trust your instinct. Discuss with your peers too.

- **Making some tough calls.** Sometimes you may have to take some hard decisions, particularly when the markets aren't performing well. There may be times when you have to compromise and not be the ethical purist you want to be. This might require making a few tough decisions, or certainly keeping your values in check so as not to cloud your judgement. For example, you may not be able to find an investment product that addresses a specific issue you are passionate about. Or perhaps you can find a fund, but it only goes part of the way. For me, I really want to plough into some of the gender equity funds that are becoming available but, honestly, I think most are way too narrowly focused. However, at the end of the day, I would rather be doing what I can with my money than not bothering at all.

- **Accepting it will take some time and energy.** The very definition of a sustainable investor requires the person to be proactive, to identify priorities and take action to achieve certain targets. This means additional time and energy from you will be required, so accept this upfront. There are ways to cut down the input required from you – such as working with a good financial advisor or joining an investment club – so finding 'partners' on your journey plays well.

## DOING GOOD WHILE MAKING MONEY

It's an outdated perception but it still exists – the myth that doing good will mean making less money. Yes, like all investment funds, there are those that outperform and there are those that don't. But many naysayers will do what they can to put you off by saying that investing sustainably leads to lower financial returns. My response to this is – be on the front foot, be armed with the evidence that blows this claim out of the water!

### What's the argument about?
Critics argue that limiting your investment portfolio by excluding certain companies that don't show 'good conduct and an adherence to certain values' might result in leaving

out some reliable performers (e.g. from the fossil fuel industry, tobacco firms and so on). They will argue that you will give up some financial performance if you put your money into a sustainable or impact investment product.

Those on the other side will counter-argue that a portfolio of companies scoring high on ESG metrics is much more likely to do well in the long run because those companies are better at managing regulatory, operational and reputational risks. We now know that non-financial factors provide important signals about future financial performance. If you are thinking through the different environmental and social issues that could impact on a company, these are likely to provide early warning signals that would not necessarily be reflected in its stock prices or financial statements.

## Look at the evidence

Let's take a look at just some of the evidence we have on the thorny topic of financial returns.

- Researchers at Morgan Stanley looked at data on nearly 11,000 mutual funds and ETFs from 2004 to 2018.[14] They found that there was in fact no financial trade-off in the returns of sustainable funds versus traditional funds. Furthermore, the research found that sustainable funds offered lower downside risk (the potential to suffer a decline in value should market conditions change). During a period of extreme volatility, sustainable funds appeared more stable in comparison to traditional funds.

- In 2016, Deutsche Asset Management and the University of Hamburg published the results of their meta-study, which aggregated evidence from more than 2,000 empirical studies on ESG and financial performance.[15] This is probably one of the most exhaustive overviews of academic research on the topic and, given its scope, allows for some generalisations to be drawn. The study showed that the business case for ESG investing is empirically very well founded. In 90 per cent of studies there was no negative relationship between ESG and financial performance and, in fact, in a large majority of studies reports were positive.

- In 2019, investment platform Willis Owen published research which revealed that 'ethical' equity indices outperform traditional ones in both the US and the UK. This trend held for both shorter- and longer-term time periods, covering one, three, five and ten years.[16]

- Most recently, in 2020, research from Morningstar assessing the long-term performance of a sample of 745 Europe-based sustainable funds showed that the majority of these strategies did better than non-ESG funds.[17] There is also evidence that ESG leaders performed better in the pandemic sell-off in early 2020.

Don't get me wrong – you will also come across data and research that align with the claims of the naysayers. However, whatever you take from the research cited above, one thing is clear – the evidence is mounting that sustainable investing is also smart investing.

## IS SUSTAINABLE INVESTING JUST FOR THE SUPER-RICH?

While we are on the topic of myths, I think this is an important one to mention – the notion that sustainable and impact investing is only the preserve of institutional investors and the super-rich. I have to admit, it probably has been this way in the past but, thankfully, this is changing.

We're starting to see the practice of sustainable investing blossom across generations, wealth brackets and asset classes.[18] This trend is important because it means that sustainable investing has the potential to be 'democratised' – so that anyone who is concerned about the state of our world and who has an active interest in using their wealth, however small or big that might be, can play a role.

We have some way to go in terms of bringing smaller investors along to the party. For example, the majority of women don't have a private banker or family office with a dedicated wealth manager, and we need to figure out how they can be adequately served. Part of this comes back to the demand and supply issue – there is a call on the financial industry to deliver sustainable investment products to the market and do more in 'selling' these, as opposed to waiting for them to be 'bought'. The more investors that get on board, the more we will have distribution at scale.

## SUSTAINABLE INVESTING AND THE QUESTIONS WE ARE ASKING

'Does capitalism need saving from itself?' was a recent headline in the *Financial Times*.[19] It is a question that truly resonates with me when I reflect on what we are really talking about when we refer to sustainable investing. I have become increasingly convinced that there is a quiet revolution happening. This revolution is posing the following questions:

1. How can the reckless, unbridled and extremely damaging behaviour of some companies go unchecked?
2. Can we reset our private sector and, as a result, push business to be a powerful tool for social good?

It is a revolution that is shining a light on the model of capitalism that we know so well – the model of capitalism that has been adopted by much of the Western world and dominated our economic systems for so long. It is a revolution that is demanding a massive overhaul of this model. At the very least, we have to recognise that capitalism hasn't been working very well. Inequality is way too high and our environmental crisis has reached a critical tipping point. Our governments seem to be incapable of acting to change this, certainly within the increasingly short time frame that looks necessary.

We have also watched large listed companies commit a whole host of sins. Whether this be failing to take responsibility or pay for the damaging externalities they create, such as air pollution or GHG emissions; or the myopic focus on short-term performance at the expense of long-term value so that they can report high quarterly profits to the market; or the quietening of the voice of employees as real wages fall and so does the workers' share in the success of the company.

## Does this mean big business to the rescue?

Big business to the rescue? Maybe. But we need to do a bit of thinking first. If businesses are to swoop in and fix big social and economic problems, we need to go back to the drawing board and think deeply about what companies are for. Here are some of the issues we would need to resolve:

- How do we make companies liable for their actions (or inactions)? We clearly have allowed companies to get away with some shocking behaviour, under the guise of profit maximisation. This has to change.

- The company bosses, the CEOs, the boards and leadership teams – they lack legitimacy and aren't accountable. How do we fix this? Do we want to fix it? Is there another model?

- How do we define 'shareholder value' and should it be replaced with the concept of 'stakeholder value'? Can this drive real change in corporate behaviour and decision-making?

- What controls do we need in place to prevent corporate leaders from using companies as political hand maidens to further their political beliefs and causes?

These questions are highlighted here to sow the seeds in your own thinking over what role you can play in building a better economic, societal and environmental system. Part of this role comes down to what you can do as an investor.

## What role does this mean investors should take?

Where is this taking us? Companies are accused of a long shopping list of wrongdoings and, by supporting these companies through investing in them, it could be argued that investors are condoning damaging corporate behaviour. Taking this on board, how does the quiet revolution apply to us?

Well, we can start by NOT investing in companies that do harm. (I feel this very, very strongly when it comes to fossil fuel companies, but I won't jump upon my personal hobby horse now.) We have an opportunity to be a new class of investor who says 'no'. No to polluting our precious Earth. No to treating people as though they have no human rights. No to corporate deceit and non-transparent behaviour.

This new class of investors can actively seek out companies that address daunting social challenges while also delivering financial returns. These companies fall into a wide array of industries and sectors – ranging from food to transportation, from healthcare to education. Just think about what we have experienced in 2020, the year when calls for racial justice have really gained steam. It is not easy and there is no quick fix but there are still ways investors can push companies to become more diverse and to stop practices that disproportionately harm certain groups based on race or ethnicity. For a start, we can choose not to invest in companies that don't align with our values.

If we band together, if we use our voice, sustainable investing will no longer be seen as some niche offering, with a label or a dedicated marketing team. No – sustainable investing will be 'just' investing. In other words, all investing will be done with sustainability priorities front and centre.

# FIVE

# CHECKING OUT THE SCENE – WHAT IS OUT THERE?

The purpose of this chapter is to help you figure out how to get started as a sustainable investor, in part by introducing some of the sustainable investment products that are emerging and turning our attention to what is actually happening in the market. To an extent, this chapter is a primer, an introduction. In terms of the nitty-gritty such as opening an investment account, do seek the support of a qualified investment professional or advisor. These chapters are for your basic knowledge but do not substitute them for expert advice.

In another note of caution before we commence – don't forget, this field is still young and has largely been the domain of the big institutional investors. For us small fish, sustainable investing hasn't really been on offer until quite recently – mainly because the financial institutions haven't seen us as a big enough market opportunity. This is changing because demand is beginning to bubble up.

# THE JOURNEY OF THE SUSTAINABLE INVESTOR

## Getting started

Now is the time to start asking yourself some fundamental questions, as you kick-start your sustainable investment journey:

1. Determine what your objectives are – your personal social and environmental priorities that will guide you. Examples might include addressing climate change or having a positive impact on local communities.
2. Taking these objectives, think about the targets you would like to set – so for climate change this could be reducing carbon emissions and seeking out offset amounts; or for local communities, creating a certain number of jobs for an underrepresented demographic.
3. Consider where you can get more information, on both your objectives and targets – you need to think this through so that you can track the impact you are having. It's not easy but worth bearing in mind as you progress.

## Top five things you should know as you get moving

- **It started small but has big ambitions.** You've seen some of the numbers already and it is clear that what started very small is now beginning to gain some significant traction. For example, in the US, ESG investments have quadrupled in the last decade.[1] This is a trend that is being observed the world over.

- **Keep it relative.** This growth is fantastic, but we are still talking about a very small proportion of overall numbers. The majority of professionally managed assets are still not falling into the sustainable camp. Just be aware of this and remember, on the upside, this means there is huge room for manoeuvre.

- **There's some serious trailblazing going on.** Women and millennials seem to be pushing the boat out for sustainable investing. Be one of them, and don't be told otherwise.

- **On trend.** All of this isn't happening in a vacuum. The world at large is prioritising action on key issues like climate change, air pollution, biodiversity, racial inequality and child labour protection. The Paris Agreement made in 2015 has set the scene for us all on climate change, and the UN Sustainable Development Goals are giving us a common language to use. No excuses.

- **Finding suitable funds.** It ain't necessarily easy, at least not yet, to find the kind of investment funds that may tick all of your boxes. Also check the fund or manager does what they say they are doing – you need to make sure that there's no greenwashing.

## PUBLIC EQUITIES FOR SUSTAINABLE INVESTORS

Public equities commonly form a core component of a well-diversified investment portfolio and, as such, investing in equities presents exciting opportunities for the sustainable investor. It's a good place to start the journey, with different ways to approach it and a range of options you can consider. What's more, as we've already talked about, the evidence is stacking up that investing in sustainable equities can produce comparable, or even improve, financial returns, particularly over the long term.

## How do you get started?

Public equity investing means you are looking for listed companies that fit your sustainability priorities. You are essentially following a conventional equity investment approach, but with a sustainability overlay. As with conventional investing, you will need to open an investing or brokerage account. Take advice from an investment professional on how and where to do this. Depending on what these are, there is a wide range of equity products available that you may want to consider.

## Single stocks

If you want to invest in single stocks (i.e. pick specific companies to invest in these directly), there are now a variety of tools and listings to help you assess how well companies perform on the sustainability or ESG scale. For example, here are some you may want to take a look at to learn more:

### S-Ray™² from Arabesque Partners

Asset manager Arabesque Partners launched S-Ray to help

investors monitor the sustainability performance of over 7,000 of the world's largest companies. S-Ray is fairly simple to use and enables you to look beneath a company's surface by assessing its non-financial performance.

It is also a technology-driven platform that builds on the power of machine learning to systematically combine a diverse set of data sources, as opposed to relying on one set of human judgements. Which is pretty cool, right?

### Corporate Knights Global 100

Corporate Knights 100 lists the 100 most sustainable corporations in the world. Created in 2005, the idea was to devise a methodology to quantitatively compare and rank the world's largest public companies. Using this methodology, all firms with a market capitalisation of at least $2 billion are considered for the listing. They are put through numerous screenings to test for key sustainability information and the top 100 are announced each year around the time of the World Economic Forum in Davos.

Both S-Ray and the Global 100 are great places to start. However, the challenge with some of the freely available tools and listings is that often the information provided is limited – for example, tools may give you only a numeric score and not much additional information on why a company has achieved that score. For additional information, you have to buy subscriptions, which can be expensive.

## Mutual funds

Instead of picking individual stocks, another option for you as a sustainable investor is to invest in a mutual fund with a clearly defined and stated sustainability strategy. This means you are looking for funds that use ESG criteria in some way to evaluate which companies to include. Sometimes these funds may pursue a sustainability-related theme or explicitly aim to create measurable social impact.

If you are thinking about investing in mutual funds, the first step is to define what you are looking for – for example, do you want to focus on a specific theme like gender equality or just generally invest in companies with robust sustainable performance? As always, once you are clear on your goals and priorities (check out Chapter 7 for some guidance on how to do this), it is recommended you speak with your financial advisor or other expert to explore available fund options and make sure you understand the potential risks involved.

## What kind of sustainable funds are there?

You will probably come across various fund 'labels' and it can be confusing, as often these include industry jargon such as:

### ESG-consideration

In general, ESG-consideration funds are those that refer to ESG criteria in their fund prospectuses (the information pack that is used to communicate with potential investors) as one set of factors that are considered in their investment process. Most of the existing funds that have recently added ESG to their prospectuses fall into this sub-group.

### ESG-integration

ESG-integration funds, by contrast, are those that make sustainability factors a major component of their processes, during both the selection of what to include and the portfolio construction. These funds also tend to be active owners, by which we mean engaging with companies and supporting (and sometimes sponsoring) ESG-related shareholder resolutions. The aim of the game is to bring about positive change within the company.

### Sustainability-themed

A third group of funds focus on broad sustainability themes and/or on delivering certain social or environmental impact alongside financial returns. These funds are devoted entirely to certain sectors and assessed against specific standards or Key Performance Indicators (KPIs). This category may also include impact funds.

For example, in recent years, we have seen a rise in the number of sustainable sector funds focusing on investment opportunities that contribute to, and aim to benefit from, the transition to a green and low-carbon economy. This is becoming increasingly topical as broader society and policy makers pay more and more attention to the need to address climate change and build climate resilient infrastructure, smart cities and so on.

## How to find sustainable funds

Many of the investor magazines are now publishing useful listings on what sustainable funds are available – so keep an eye out for market-specific ideas. Any examples given here are just that – examples! By no means am I providing any recommendations, I am just citing a few examples that I have come across in the course of my research and making my own investment decisions. Also be aware that where you live will define which funds are available to you. Frustratingly, some markets, such as Europe, have more to offer than others.

It is also worth checking with your bank to find out what it offers. For example, Standard Chartered Bank seems to be doing some interesting stuff for retail investors wanting to get into sustainable investing.[3] The bank now offers a number of investment options – from sustainable funds (mutual funds that incorporate good ESG principles) to stocks of companies which publicise what they are doing in the ESG space.[4]

Standard Chartered Private Bank has also introduced some specific products that cater to high-net-worth individuals, such as the Impact Philosophy app which supports investors in figuring out the sectors or industries they want to invest in to make an impact. Once the user defines their priorities, the private bank helps with what type of investment opportunity may be suitable – possibly even private equity products or direct investments.

In another example, Morgan Stanley Wealth Management now runs a series of 'impact portfolios' through which investors can choose the approach they want in order to achieve the impact they seek. These actively managed portfolios can be set up or tilted towards several themes, such as those included in the Sustainable Development Goals such as 'climate action'. To address these requirements, the bank then makes available mutual funds and ETFs investing in companies that are tackling these issues.

## Other sources of information

You might also find investment listings for retail investors through your national or regional sustainable or responsible investment association (essentially a trade body or industry association promoting the industry and the broader ecosystem). For example, in Canada, the Responsible Investment Association hosts the RI Marketplace, a useful listing of investment products, investment advisors and service providers.[5]

In Australia and New Zealand, RIAA (Responsible Investment Association Australasia) offers an investment certification programme, aimed at helping investors figure out which investment options and financial advice best match their investment beliefs and personal values. By providing consistent and standardised information, it helps investors compare and contrast their options. Responsible Returns (Australia) also has a search function to find responsible or ethical banking, superannuation and investment products that match values and interests.

I do admit, it is not always easy to find accessible information, particularly aimed at retail investors, which does put quite a lot of the onus on you to do the legwork. That said, there are often listings or databases which, while intended for the financial industry, can provide food for thought as you start your sustainable investment journey.

For example, in the UK, Fund EcoMarket is a database aimed at intermediaries (the middleperson in a financial transaction) but is open to anyone and everyone. Information on the website is not to be regarded as financial advice (not least because it is not regulated as such) but it's a good place to go for more information on sustainable funds. It is primarily for people based in the UK, but you can use the geographic and regional filter to find funds with international strategies. Another example of an industry database is Global Fund Search, which now offers a list of sustainable fund 'leaders' – such as the Leaders Universe Sustainable Equity.

Morningstar offers investors investment research such as fund, stock and general market data. In 2016, the firm introduced Morningstar's Sustainability Ratings – a system for rating whether an investment is well positioned against its peers. Many use this rating system as a reliable and objective way to see how approximately 20,000 mutual funds and ETFs are meeting their ESG challenges.

The good news is that there is a big drive in different markets for greater ESG transparency and some of the big players are really getting behind this trend. For example, in 2020, MSCI made public ESG metrics for all of its EU regulated indexes, mutual funds and ETFs. This move is part of a bigger ESG transparency initiative to provide consistent and comparable ESG metrics at the company, fund and index level. Basically, if you are on the MSCI website you can access search tools to look at ESG ratings and metrics. This is a big move forward.[6]

## ETFS FOR SUSTAINABLE INVESTORS

We talked earlier about exchange-traded funds and their rising popularity for many retail investors. Today there is a relatively wide range of ETFs available that consider or reflect sustainability strategies or priorities. This is an exciting development because it helps smaller investors get into the sustainable investing space. Why? Because ETFs tend to be much more accessible, lower in cost than other investment options, and offer an easier way to diversify while catering to certain environmental and social goals.

As with mutual funds, you will find a range of funds which vary in the type of investment strategy used to obtain the sustainability label. This may include:

- Excluding from the ETF certain companies or sectors based on specific ESG criteria – this is called negative or exclusionary screening. An example is the MSCI Global Socially Responsible Indices, which exclude companies involved in alcohol, gambling, tobacco, military weapons and other unsustainable activities.

- In contrast, positive or best-in-class screening involves choosing to invest in sectors, companies or projects selected for positive sustainability performance relative to industry peers. Companies scoring highly on ESG criteria are given a higher weight in the index. For instance, Company A will receive a relatively higher weight than Company B if Company A's ESG score is higher than Company B's.

- In particular, we are now seeing the development of more thematically focused 'sustainable ETFs'. A few examples of some of the bigger theme-based ETFs (size based on assets under management) include Invesco Water Resources ETF, SPDR S&P North American Natural Resources ETF and Invesco Solar ETF.

## Some examples of sustainable ETFs

As with general ETFs, there are now a large number of ETFs popping up specifically for sustainable investors. Many of the financial media providers such as Yahoo Finance are running lists that make it easier to find out what is out there – but here are a few examples available at the time of writing. Of course, availability also depends on what country or market you are in and therefore what is available to you.

### Fidelity Sustainable World ETF

A global equity strategy that invests in companies with strong ESG performance. Fidelity also offers a mutual fund version of the ETF that expands access and choice for financial advisors and investors.

### Vanguard ESG US Stock ETF

This ESG fund is based on a large group of holdings with some 1,500 total components. Focusing on US companies with above-average ESG ratings, it also includes some smaller companies because of the depth of the line-up of stocks. Some investors like this because it gives them exposure to smaller stocks from across the American economy.

### SPDR S&P 500 Fossil Fuel Reserves Free ETF

An interesting option is this ETF that excludes all the oil, gas and fossil fuel companies out of the popular S&P 500 index list of stocks. It leaves the investor with a large number of stocks while excluding the fossil fuel-based energy majors.

### BlackRock's iShares

BlackRock has a $60 billion platform of dedicated sustainable investment solutions. Of particular interest may be iShares – a family of exchange-traded funds managed by BlackRock. For example, iShares ESG MSCI EAFE ETF offers a more global approach than some of the ETFs listed above because it excludes companies in the US and Canada. It is an interesting one to consider because some companies in regions such as Europe are more progressive in their ESG activities.

## BONDS FOR SUSTAINABLE INVESTORS

Sustainable bonds are fixed income projects with fixed returns, essentially loans used to finance projects that bring about clear environmental and social-economic benefits. Interestingly, studies have shown the positive effect that ESG investing can also have on bond portfolio performance.[7] As an investor, you can invest in a bond fund or bond ETF, so keep these options in mind as you explore what is available in your market.

Before you invest in a sustainable bond fund or bond ETF, as always try to be clear on whether it supports your sustainable investment goals. For example, if you really care about healthcare, nutrition or childhood development, you might want to take a closer look at the emerging 'social development bonds'. However, if environmental factors lie close to your heart, you may want to focus more on the 'green bonds' sector.

- Green bonds: these are defined as loans used to finance projects and activities that are climate-related or specifically benefit the environment. These projects may include development of renewable energy production, or green transportation, or an energy efficiency project. In recent years, we have seen a boom in the number of green bonds, although these have primarily been available to institutional investors. It is definitely harder for individual investors like you and me to get into bonds, but this is changing.

- Impact bonds (or social development bonds): once again, loans that are made on the basis of certain social benefits to be achieved by the service provider. Often impact bonds involve three parties – private investors, the public sector or donors, and the service provider, which is a non-profit organisation. These types of bonds were originally created to improve the efficiency of social services and it may be that these instruments provide an additional source of funds for social impact that cannot be achieved by a company.

## A few examples of sustainable bonds

While there are still only a limited number of sustainable bonds available to retail investors, there is an increasing number coming onto the market, which is great news.

If you are interested in green bonds, you may be able to access a green bond fund. A few that exist include Mirova Global Green Bond Fund, Calvert Green Bond Fund and VanEck Vectors Green Bond ETF, which tracks the S&P Green Bond US Dollar Select Index.

On a themed sustainable bond, take a look at the Women's Livelihood Bond (WLB), issued by the Impact Investment Exchange (IIX). The bond won the 2019 UN Global Action Award, an award scheme that recognises some of the most innovative, scalable and replicable solutions aimed at tackling climate change alongside other Sustainable Development Goals.

While still only available to accredited investors, the $150 million WLB is a great example of using innovative finance to help create sustainable livelihoods for millions of women across Asia. The WLB series basically pools together a group of impact enterprises to issue a collective bond. It's different from some of the more traditional social impact bonds in that it also aims to mobilise private sector capital to generate positive social impact at the same time as offering financial returns.

## PRIVATE EQUITY FOR SUSTAINABLE INVESTORS

Over the last couple of years, some of the biggest and best-known private equity firms have begun to get more serious about sustainable investment and ESG practices. This is happening because smart managers see the value that managing sustainability risks can bring, particularly when the firm exits (when the investee company is sold). This sector shift has also come about because of strong client demand from investors who recognise it is not necessary to trade off financial return for positive societal and environmental impact.

Given typical investment timelines, PE firms are well positioned to hold long-term perspectives and care about long-term outcomes, making them ideal sustainable investors. In addition, PE firms often buy controlling stakes in companies, with a board seat included, and so can exert influence to make the kind of changes needed to implement sustainability strategies and projects.

With all that said, unfortunately for individual investors like us, it can be difficult to get exposure to this asset class as the required minimum investments tend to be very high (i.e. $1 million, $5 million or more).

That said, many individuals will have exposure through their pension funds as today many of these funds include private equity in their portfolio mix. It is worth taking a look at what private equity holdings your pension fund may have.

### Examples of sustainable private equity funds

Interestingly, some PE firms have also begun to design 'impact strategies' and launched funds on the back of these – such as TPG's Rise Fund, Bain Capital's Double Impact and KKR's Global Impact. These types of funds have a well-established process and are increasingly good at assessing impact and measuring progress.

The private equity sector plays a critical role in raising the level of funding needed to achieve the Sustainable Development Goals by 2030. It will be interesting to watch this space evolve and perhaps offer more to retail investors at a future date.

## CROWDFUNDING FOR SUSTAINABLE INVESTORS

Crowdfunding has grown rapidly from a Silicon Valley social experiment to a multi-billion-dollar industry. And this astounding growth looks set to continue – with annual volumes expected to reach $100 billion by 2025. This means crowdfunding is becoming the leading funding channel for small and medium-sized enterprises (SMEs).

Of particular note is how crowdfunding is taking hold in developing countries, with India, the Philippines and Nepal being some of the emerging market leaders.

Crowdfunding – with its ability to bring in smaller investors and act as a much more inclusive and democratic asset class – is ripe for investors who are also driven by social and environmental priorities. So how do you find interesting and sustainable projects in this fast-growing market?

## How do you get involved?

To date, it seems that it's easiest to get into crowdfunding from the environmental angle. Most of the major crowdfunding platforms now have a specific environmental section where you can find different types of green projects. If this piques your interest, you might want to start by taking a look at the main crowdfunding platforms to see what their offerings are for green finance.

Take a look at Kickstarter, which has a category called Go Green where 'sustainable campaigns' are listed. Indiegogo has a similar category called Environment. Examples of companies and projects you could invest in through these platforms include a solar driven cell phone charger, environmentally responsible sandals, turning poo into power in Pakistan and much more!

## Tailored sustainable investment crowdfunding platforms

Crowdfunding platforms with a specific focus on sustainability are still at an early stage – but momentum is growing. These platforms allow investors to seek out sustainable projects and drive change through investing directly. A couple of examples include EcoCrowd and GreenCrowd. Many of these platforms are still quite small and more locally focused, but over time they have great potential to develop and play a much more transformative role.

## ANGEL INVESTING FOR SUSTAINABLE INVESTORS

For the sustainable investor, angel investing is an exciting field because it opens up access to capital for innovative companies at the forefront of addressing major social or environmental challenges. Angel investing can be a powerful tool for scaling businesses that are designed to make money while also having a measurable social impact.

### Is angel investing for you as a sustainable investor?

Here are a few thoughts you may want to consider before launching into angel investing as a sustainable investor:

- It is very personal and therefore fairly easy to align with your values because you can carefully select companies that sit within your identified strategy or sustainability priorities.

- Depending on your investment size, you may be able to play an active role in ensuring that the company stays aligned with its mission. This is where getting your hands dirty can really help.

- The feel-good factor is undeniable – when you are positioned close to a business that is looking to make a difference, it can be an amazing feeling. You can experience that sense of collective purpose, knowing that you are working alongside people with similar values and priorities.

- As we know, angel or early-stage investing is risky. On the upside, companies can generate large financial returns while also helping innovative businesses to address some of the most critical social and environmental problems. On the downside, some or indeed many of the sustainability-related companies you might look at may have business propositions based on unproven business models or untested technologies.

- However, it is important to remember that companies delivering positive social or environmental impacts that are addressing today's current challenges stand a chance of making business sense in our future world, and if so, can potentially outperform in the long term.

- It takes a long time to build a company. So, as an early investor you need to be prepared to wait a long time until you are likely to reap any financial return (usually when the company is sold, or when it goes public). You are probably looking at five to 10 years – but be prepared that the returns horizon may extend beyond this, particularly if the company you are investing in is experimenting with innovative business models or developing markets. Sometimes people refer to this as 'patient capital' for a good reason.

- We face challenges in measuring our success as angel investors beyond the financials, as we still have minimal data on early-stage companies that are also seeking positive social and/or environmental impact. Of course, this presents the opportunity to work with the company (investee) to establish impact measurement frameworks that perhaps include regular reporting with qualitative and quantitative metrics. Bear in mind, this needs to be useful and not bring more administrative burden to a small company.

## WHERE DO INDICES SIT IN ALL OF THIS?

You might have heard people talk about a stock market index or perhaps an index fund. A stock market index is, in its simplest form, a measurement of a section of the stock market. It represents a way or a tool that is used by investors and fund managers to 'describe' the market. It is used to compare the return on a specific investment or investments. Indices can be classified in different ways:

- 'Global' indices such as the S&P Global 100 or the MSCI World include stocks from certain regions (e.g. Europe, Asia) or levels of income or industrialisation (e.g. emerging markets).

- 'National' indices represent the stock market of a given nation and are used to reflect investor sentiment on the state of that nation's economy. These include often quoted indices that are made up of stocks of large companies listed on a country's largest stock exchange such as the British FTSE 100, Japanese Nikkei 225 and the American S&P 500.

- Not all indices are linked to exchanges and we are also seeing specialised indices that track the performance of specific sectors of the market such as the Morgan Stanley Biotech Index, which comprises US firms in the biotechnology industry, or the S&P Global BMI Shariah Index, which is geared towards investors who adhere to Islamic laws.

### Are index funds the same as mutual funds or ETFs?

A lot of mutual funds and exchange-traded funds attempt to 'track' a particular index and are called (unsurprisingly) index funds. The fund will include a portfolio constructed to match or track the components of a specified market index.

These can be a good option because they provide broad market exposure and often have low operating expenses. For this reason, they are often considered important for core portfolio holdings for pensions and retirement accounts.

The differences lie in how you buy them. Investors purchase ETFs directly from a stock exchange through a brokerage. Index funds can be bought directly from a fund company.

### Enter the sustainability index

There is a wide range of sustainability indices – many of which are used to determine how sustainable a company's performance is. This is then compared against the sustainability performance of other companies in a given region, sector or globally. For example, a sustainability index may exclude companies on the basis of specific industries such as nuclear or conventional weapons production, the tobacco industry or the fossil fuel industry. On the other hand, a sustainability index may rate companies for inclusion based on, for example, their environmental and/or sustainability performance, supply chain standards or relationships with external stakeholders.

Here are a few examples of indices and index funds:

- STOXX Global ESG Leaders Index – represents the leading global companies based on ESG criteria.

- The Dow Jones Sustainability™ World Index comprises global sustainability leaders as identified by SAM. It represents the top 10 per cent of the largest 2,500 companies in the S&P Global BMI based on long-term economic, environmental and social criteria.

- FTSE4Good Index Series – a series of stock market indices and benchmarks that include companies based on a range of ESG criteria.

## DOING THIS IN PRACTICE

### What's available, what's not
I won't lie – what is available to the average investor isn't extensive or unlimited. It will take some work on your

part, along with support from your bank, advisor or investment club, to find out what is available to you given the market you are in.

This is changing as demand from retail investors continues to grow. If you can't find anything, start pushing financial institutions on why they are not providing sustainable investment products to people like you and me. Only by speaking up will our voice be heard.

## What kind of growth are we seeing?

For investors like us, the number of sustainable funds is undoubtedly on the up. Hopefully this trend will mean that we start to see many more options become available for retail investors.

On ETFs with sustainability goals, we are definitely seeing these take off. According to BlackRock, the world's largest asset management firm, sustainable ETFs are positioned to grow to $400 billion by 2028.[8]

## What is in your pension?

One of the first places to start is looking at your existing pension fund, as this is likely to be your primary existing investment pot and it may well be that you have no idea what is lurking there.

In some markets, pension funds have become strong advocates for responsible and sustainable investment practices. For example, since 2017, Japan's Government Pension Investment Fund, the world's largest pension fund, has set out to become a market leader on responsible and sustainable investment. In 2018, New York City announced that its public pension funds would be divesting $5 billion from fossil fuel companies within five years. Take a look at how your pension fund is invested – does it live up to your expectations on sustainability issues? If not, can you contact its managers to push for progress?

That said, always be aware of greenwashing. I recall a few years back when I was living in Hong Kong and I was invested in the mandatory pension scheme. I had automatically checked the 'green fund' box, assuming I would be putting my money in renewables, green technologies and other innovations that would be helping us to address the environmental challenges we are facing. It took me a couple of years to double-check and I found that I was actually investing in a large investment bank that was heavily financing the coal industry in Asia. It had only been included in the pension fund on the basis of factors like office paper usage. A financial institution is bound to have a low carbon footprint if you only look at its direct operations! Perhaps the fund methodology should have used other criteria against which to measure the ESG performance of the companies it included. Classic example of greenwashing.

## Passive investing – what's all the fuss?

You may well have heard about passive investing and wondered what all the fuss was about. Passive investing is essentially an investment strategy which aims to maximise returns by minimising buying and selling. Index investing is one of the most common forms of passive investing, because investors are purchasing a benchmark and holding over a long period, keeping transaction costs minimal.

People like passive investing because not a lot of trading is done so fees are low. Proponents also argue that it takes emotion out of investing as decisions are not based on market sentiment or fears.

When it comes to sustainable investing, there has been some debate around the extent to which passive investing can fit. Because sustainable investing requires that the investor select companies based on certain positive social or environmental impact or return, there is undoubtedly some conflict. If you get into index investing, it could be argued that you are 'buying the market' and not choosing companies based on certain business practices or sustainability performance. It's not a discretionary process.

That said, we have seen an increasing proliferation of sustainable investment products within the passive investment space, leveraging ESG factors in passive strategies. For the sustainable investor, these products offer easy access. If you want to learn more about the debate, I highly recommend reading the Principles for Responsible Investment's discussion paper, *How Can a Passive Investor Be a Responsible Investor?*[9]

## SOME FINAL THOUGHTS

It's important to be a sceptical buyer. We're not immune from the temptation to be brought in by exaggerated claims. So, as you think about your sustainable investment strategy and consider specific investment routes and funds, bear in mind the following questions you may want to ask:

### Is it aligned with my values?

Sustainable investing is not an exact science and it is not always black and white. Just something to be aware of. For example, if you choose to go into an index fund that uses an ESG weighting to consider companies for inclusion, you could still end up investing in a sector you don't want to be in.

You might also want to check out whether a fund manager actively engages with companies – by this, we are talking about fund managers who are proactive in engaging with companies on specific ESG issues with the intention of having a positive impact in a way that enhances the company's long-term strength and performance.

### Are these investments costing me more?

Historically, any special investment strategy has usually incurred higher fees, and this has probably held true for sustainable investment products too. You are essentially paying for someone to do the research on companies for you, so it does make sense. That said, fees have fallen dramatically but be aware of this as you make any investment decisions.

## What are you measuring against?

Of course, you will want to evaluate how you are doing and benchmarks often help with this. Benchmarks have been developed by the industry to evaluate the risks and rewards of an investment. However, when it comes to sustainable investing, these traditional benchmarks might not be hugely useful. In fact, they can be misleading for the sustainable investor.

# SIX

# A GLOBAL CALL TO ACTION – INTRODUCING THE SUSTAINABLE DEVELOPMENT GOALS

I have mentioned the Sustainable Development Goals (SDGs) several times already. So, let's take a moment to delve into them properly, exploring what they are and how investors like us can leverage them as a framework to organise our own thinking. They do not have to form a rigid framework, rather a tool that might help you on your sustainable investment journey.

The SDGs have now evolved into a 'global call to action' and their influence is reaching all corners of the world. This is significant because, even in the mainstream financial industry, we are starting to see people talk about the SDGs, to use them for structuring products as well as defining outcomes and impact.

# WHAT ARE THE SUSTAINABLE DEVELOPMENT GOALS?

The United Nations Sustainable Development Goals are a collection of 17 objectives aimed at improving the overall quality of life in the world by 2030.[1] In a nutshell, the SDGs represent the closest thing we have to a 'world strategy' because they provide a clear and structured approach to thinking about global challenges. For this reason, they can provide a useful framework for thinking about our own sustainable investment priorities and decisions. Don't get me wrong – the SDGs won't do the work for you, but they can certainly help you on your way.

### How did the SDGs come about?

Back in 2012, at the United Nations Conference on Sustainable Development in Rio de Janeiro, the SDGs were born – or rather, the process of replacing the Millennium Development Goals (MDGs) was hatched. It took until 2015 for the SDGs finally to be agreed and adopted.

The MDGs had been about tackling the indignity of poverty with measurable, universally agreed objectives covering extreme poverty and hunger, preventing deadly diseases and expanding primary education, alongside other development priorities.

The SDGs expanded this, intending to produce a set of universal goals designed to meet the urgent political, governance, economic, environmental and social challenges facing the world.

A certain amount of cynicism surrounds discussion on what the MDGs achieved but it should also be recognised that they did play an essential role in: lifting more than a billion people out of extreme poverty; reducing child mortality by more than half; reducing the number of out-of-school children by more than half; bringing HIV/AIDS infections down by almost 40 per cent.[2]

Thinking positively, the legacy of the MDGs teaches us much about the importance of setting global goals, towards which we can all work. Yet while the achievements were admirable, the job remains unfinished, and when we look at where we stand today, there is much work still to be done. The SDGs build on the MDGs by bringing in the other critical dimensions of sustainable development.

## What do the SDGs cover?

At the heart of the 2030 Agenda for Sustainable Development sit the 17 Sustainable Development Goals. These are as follows:

- GOAL 1: No Poverty

- GOAL 2: Zero Hunger

- GOAL 3: Good Health and Well-being

- GOAL 4: Quality Education

- GOAL 5: Gender Equality

- GOAL 6: Clean Water and Sanitation

- GOAL 7: Affordable and Clean Energy

- GOAL 8: Decent Work and Economic Growth

- GOAL 9: Industry, Innovation and Infrastructure

- GOAL 10: Reduced Inequalities

- GOAL 11: Sustainable Cities and Communities

- GOAL 12: Responsible Consumption and Production

- GOAL 13: Climate Action

- GOAL 14: Life Below Water

- GOAL 15: Life on Land

- GOAL 16: Peace, Justice and Strong Institutions

- GOAL 17: Partnerships for the Goals

Quite an ambitious list, eh? And it doesn't stop there. Underpinning the 17 Goals sit 169 targets, and under each target there are between one and three indicators intended to measure progress towards reaching the targets. In total, there are 232 approved indicators.[3] Obviously, a great deal of thinking went into defining the SDGs and, for this reason, it makes a lot of sense to leverage the framework. The Goals provide us with a common language, so let's use it.

There are a few other important features of the SDGs worth a mention:

- **Interconnectedness.** This may be obvious, but the SDGs are closely connected with one another, drawing in multiple cross-cutting issues. One of the best examples is gender equality, in particular how achieving this can positively impact on many other SDGs.

- **SDG-driven investment.** Achieving the SDGs requires significant investment and it probably represents the most ambitious financing strategy for sustainable development yet. This will come from public resources but also private investment (you and me!). Pension funds will also play an important role. Why? Pension funds have the long-term mandate to manage the retirement funds of people all over the world. Clients of pension funds have a dual interest – to enjoy a decent pension, while also living in a just, fair and peaceful society. In light of this, you might want to take a look at what your pension fund is doing on the SDGs.

- **Entrepreneurship.** Progress towards achieving the SDGs will require empowering dedicated and innovative entrepreneurs to build businesses and provide products and services that help create a world with fewer inequalities and injustices. As investors, we can play our part in supporting these businesses, particularly those with a social and impact objective.

## SDGs and women

Given this book is for women, I would be remiss if I didn't shine a spotlight on what the SDGs could mean for women across the world. Gender equality gets its very own SDG – SDG 5: 'Achieve gender equality and empower all women and girls' – but it is also woven throughout the SDGs framework – including healthcare, education, livelihoods and far beyond.

SDG 5 has clearly articulated targets such as ending all forms of discrimination against women and girls everywhere; ensuring women's full and effective participation in decision-making in political, economic and public life; and ensuring universal access to sexual and reproductive health.

Despite woeful progress, we need to hit these targets by 2030. Did you know that, at the time of writing, in 18 countries, husbands can legally prevent their wives from working? In 39 countries, daughters and sons do not have equal inheritance rights? And 49 countries lack laws protecting women from domestic violence?[4]

It's not just a moral argument. Evidence clearly demonstrates that investing in women and girls is closely linked to boosting economic growth, reducing inequalities and strengthening financial resilience for families and communities.[5] Furthermore, given women's leadership on sustainability, I would argue that empowering more and more women will drive exponential growth in the number of people who want to have a positive impact and make a difference in the world. For these reasons, investing with a gender lens is a fascinating field and I will run through it all in greater depth in Chapter 10.

## WHY DO THE SDGS MATTER?

Yes, the SDGs do have some pretty lofty aims such as zero hunger, quality education, gender equality and no poverty. At first sight, it might seem that using the SDGs for your investment strategy is overly ambitious, certainly challenging to say the least. But there are many ways in which the SDG framework is driving change.

## Within companies

We've already talked about ESG, and for many companies, embracing ESG has also meant adopting the 17 Sustainable Development Goals. These Goals don't talk about cutting business costs or expanding profits, but instead about how enterprises can make an environmental and societal impact while still pursuing their business aims.

Some companies are genuinely aligning their strategies to the SDGs, as well as putting in place ways to measure and manage their contribution to the Goals' realisation.[6] There's also a lot of talk around building inclusive businesses and how the SDGs play a role in this, linking back to our previous discussion on the purpose of companies.

If you are interested in digging deeper into how companies are moving forward on the SDGs, take a look at the work of the UN Global Compact.[7] This initiative is all about aligning the strategies and operations of companies across the world with principles on human and labour rights, environment, anti-corruption and other societal goals. It also showcases what various business leaders are doing so you can see the global goals in action.

## To investors

In the last couple of years, we have seen a large number of institutional investors and financial institutions talk seriously about sustainable development and the role that they play in achieving the SDGs. I am firmly of the view that the financial industry can and should be doing more but it's heartening to see how many players are now focusing on the SDGs.

From the investor perspective, this is driven by a number of factors and it is certainly because many believe that companies focused on achieving the SDGs, companies with a keen awareness and action on sustainable development priorities, will likely be the most financially profitable in the long run. Why? There are many reasons. These companies are prepared for the future, aware of the risks but also how the world is transforming. They are also attracting the best talent to drive this transformation.

## To you

I look at sustainable investing like this – what is the world going to look like tomorrow? With all the challenges and difficulties that we are facing today – whether it's climate change, environmental damage, concern about labour rights, the massive gender disparity in all fields of life – we know that change has to happen.

The SDGs provide us with the direction of travel. This is what we aspire to, this is where we are heading. It aligns with thinking about new ways of doing things. So as individual investors, you and I can also align with this new way of thinking, by investing in companies and sectors that are actively working towards achieving these Goals.

Tomorrow's world will not be filled with companies that are non-sustainable, whose value is based on dead assets that cause huge risk or face potential litigation further down the line. Those companies will be excluded from our investment support as they do not provide for the kind of future world we want to build and pass on. One thing that the COVID-19 pandemic has taught us is that we urgently need an effective framework to deal with global problems.

## ARE WE ON TRACK TO ACHIEVE THE SDGS BY 2030?

It's clear that we still have a long, long way to go on the SDGs, with progress insufficient to meet the 2030 targets, and advancements uneven across individual Goals and countries. Take gender equality – at the current pace, no one country is on track to achieve this by 2030.[8] And while in general, people are living healthier and happier lives, wars and climate change are resulting in forced migration and a rise in world hunger.

Given this serious concern that we are off track, the discussion is increasingly moving from the 'why' to the 'how'. This is occurring both in the corporate and financial worlds. A few years back this was not the case because many CEOs and investors were wary of UN bureaucracy and attaching their names and brands to the institution. This has fundamentally shifted, and we are seeing more and more companies, more and more corporate leaders, pledge to take action on the SDGs.

That said, it is still proving challenging for many senior leaders to direct their organisations to support the SDGs. We're still seeing a great deal of effort needed on defining standards, designing corporate processes and measuring progress.

There is a good deal of hope, however, in the efforts of many vital non-governmental organisations like the UN Global Compact and the World Benchmarking Alliance and other initiatives which are pushing corporates to work out detailed SDG plans and metrics. And this in turn is feeding into the financial industry.

## WHAT IS THE FINANCIAL INDUSTRY DOING ON THE SDGS?

It is estimated that between $5 and $7 trillion will be needed annually until 2030 to achieve the SDGs. The World Bank estimates that 50–80 per cent of the funding will come from domestic governments – which means the remainder must come from investors. We have our work cut out!

At the same time, this is also a massive opportunity for the financial industry to reframe its role, through engaging in sustainable development and embedding sustainability principles against which to operate. Admittedly, progress has been slow, but we are seeing some at the forefront of the industry really taking hold of the SDGs. Here are some examples of what's happening, demonstrating that it's not just empty talk.

## Tribe Impact Capital

As impact wealth managers, Tribe works with its clients to help them identify, understand and articulate their values and the positive change they want to create in the world. They do this by using the UN SDGs as the 'impact lens' to create what Tribe calls a client's ImpactDNA™. This provides each client with a unique set of markers that can be used to craft a tailored and personal strategy for managing their wealth.

Tribe describes this as a pioneering new approach to wealth management and certainly its goal to deliver long-term positive impact and growth for everyone, in support of the SDGs, is winning admiration and accolades. I highly recommend reading Tribe's recent impact report, which shares how it is doing as a business and how it is working with its clients.[9] It also describes how Tribe translates the UN SDGs into four macro impact investment themes, as well as introducing some of the impact metrics it uses to measure progress – in this case carbon equivalency as a measure of how aligned its investments are with the Paris Agreement.

## SDG Invest

SDG Invest is a mutual fund offered to private and institutional investors, investing in listed companies that are addressing global challenges through fulfilling the SDGs. Companies are selected through a three-step process:

1. Financial selection (first, performing financial due diligence on each company)
2. Sectoral selection (second, using a negative screening process to exclude companies from certain sectors)
3. SDG screening (finally, using SDG Invest's Sustainability Scorecard)

This process certainly whittles down the number of companies eligible for inclusion but, as corporate leaders begin to do more on the SDG agenda, it is likely the number of companies will increase in years to come.

## SDG Impact Bond for Livelihood

In 2019, Grameen Impact and Acumen launched an SDG bond for 'for-profit' social enterprises in India. The idea is to support sustainable livelihoods for youth in rural and urban areas in the country, through creating a structure that allows private investors and corporates to invest in a debt financing structure that focuses on impact outcomes.

## Robeco SDG Credit Funds

RobecoSAM, one of the first asset managers to launch an SDG equity product, has also launched an SDG credits product. It is a fixed income fund that applies a screening process to select issuers that contribute to realising the

SDGs. It also excludes issuers that contribute negatively to these Goals.

## Standard Chartered Bank Green and Sustainable Product Framework

Standard Chartered has a useful document which outlines the bank's view on green and sustainable products, setting out qualifying themes and activities. In the document these are also mapped against their relevant SDGs and SDG targets. It is a useful read because the 'Impact Framework' is helpful in drilling down on different SDGs and what is considered in versus out.

# WHERE NOW? USING THE SDGS TO DEFINE YOUR INVESTMENT STRATEGY

SDGs can be used as a reference point to illustrate the relationship between your investments and your intended goals. It is not a perfect model, but it is a framework that can help organise your thinking and categorise your decisions.

It is important to explore how to set your sustainable investment strategy and objectives, and how these can fit around the SDGs. So let's take some time to look into the SDGs in more detail and figure out which ones really matter to you.

## A heads up – the risk of SDG washing

Greenwashing, impact washing, SDG washing... as these concepts rise in popularity so too does the risk that people, companies and funds are branding themselves as having a positive impact in this space, when the reality is this may not be the case. We run the risk that investment products use labels as marketing tools. The result of empty promises is damage to the reputation of the sustainable investment industry. Be aware of this and do as much of your own due diligence as you can. Perhaps more and more, we need global standards so that sustainable investors can know what they are buying, and the industry can be underpinned by transparency.

### AMY CLARKE, CO-FOUNDER AND CHIEF IMPACT OFFICER, TRIBE IMPACT CAPITAL

*Tribe Impact Capital LLP (Tribe) is the UK's first dedicated Impact Wealth Manager, created in response to a significant increase in demand from individuals and charities wanting to achieve both sustainable impact and a financial return from their invested wealth. Tribe aims to fill the advice gap for those who want to achieve a positive social impact with their wealth by offering a full discretionary and advisory portfolio management service focusing only on those assets that do so.*

**Why are the UN SDGs such a powerful tool for investors?**

The UN SDGs define the safe space needed for everyone and everything to thrive. They form a universally accepted framework which, while being predominantly created as a public policy tool, allows investors to identify and address the key social, economic AND environmental issues facing society, now and through to 2030, and beyond. They are the closest thing we have to a crystal ball in terms of what the future could and should look like and clearly outline the risks and the opportunities associated with inaction and action. They are the fundamental drivers of sustainable development, and, therefore, underpin the breadth and depth of future economic growth. This makes them an incredibly powerful tool for investors.

**How can a woman get started in terms of using the UN SDGs to frame her investment thinking?**

Thinking about the change you want to see in the world is a good start. Everybody has a unique set of personal values and passions as well as financial objectives. The 17 UN SDGs provide an incredibly effective framework to align your values, your financial aspirations and the change you want to see in the world – your impact. They are also a great tool to help screen the investment universe to identify the businesses that reflect your values and the change you are seeking to create. We know women are particularly predisposed to patient capital and also often engage more in conscious or caring capital. The UN SDGs help women understand more about their financial preferences as they relate to their values and, therefore, help us all better understand where we want to invest, in what, and over what period of time.

# PART II

PART II

# SEVEN

# DON'T BE PUT OFF –
# THE TIME IS NOW

Becoming a sustainable investor can seem like a daunting task, but don't be put off. This chapter is designed to support you in starting your journey. Where you put your money matters: it should reflect your beliefs and it should be integral to your personal philosophy. Don't accept anything less.

So far, we have covered the concept of sustainable investing – what it is and why it matters. I've introduced you to the basics of investing and the different investment options that are available. I've shown you that the principles of sustainable investing are increasingly being applied to traditional investment products and asset classes. Finally, we've taken a look at the Sustainable Development Goals and how these can be used as a potential framework for thinking through what matters to you.

Investors are increasingly embracing sustainable investing. Take courage that it can be done but, at the same time, recognise that there is no one-size-fits-all approach. Sustainable investing means different things to different people and your own beliefs, goals and strategy can vary considerably from the next woman.

It is also important to know that, while many in the investment industry may find it easy to talk about sustainability, it is more challenging for them to implement this in their approach. We talk more about the challenges in the next chapter. That said, it doesn't mean that it can't be done and, with this in mind, we now run through a simple pathway for you to follow.[1]

## PRIORITISE WHAT YOU CARE ABOUT

One of the best ways to start your sustainable investing journey is by identifying your priorities – the issues you really care about. What sort of world do you want to live in? Where do you want to see change happen? This will require some soul searching as well as an appreciation that it may not be possible to fix everything at once.

Ask yourself – what kind of issues are important to me? Here are some examples:

- Buying clothes knowing that the workers who have made them have been treated fairly and paid equitably.

- Knowing that a company works closely with local communities, perhaps through helping them to secure their water supply or supporting local schools.

- Purchasing an electric vehicle because you want to reduce your contribution to air pollution.

- Seeking out companies that are actively looking to reduce their carbon footprint by reducing their GHG emissions.

You can see where I'm going with this, right? Now write a list of your own top 10 priorities – the environmental and social issues that are most important to you, whether that is combating air pollution or eradicating forced labour (or perhaps both!). Once you have this mapped out on paper, you will be able to take the next step.

## If you are struggling

Perhaps you may not be able to list off causes you passionately want to support. However, the chances are that you do know the types of industries and companies that you want nothing to do with – for example, this may include the coal industry or weapon manufacturers. Because of the large number of options, this may be a good place to start. In the investment world, this is called 'negative screening' and can be a sensible way to get started.

## Loop back to the Sustainable Development Goals

This is also where you may want to revisit the SDGs. The 17 Goals pretty much cover every aspect of our societal, economic and environmental lives. Drill down to the target level that sits under each of the Goals because this will help you understand the specifics of what you might want to include in your priority listing. This level of granularity can help you think through the kind of impacts or outcomes you want to achieve.

## TRANSLATE YOUR PRIORITIES INTO SUSTAINABLE INVESTMENT BELIEFS

Having a better understanding of your priorities can then help you to plot your sustainable investment beliefs.

### What are sustainable investment beliefs?

These are the guiding principles that spell out who you are and what you want to achieve with your investments. To put it another way, your sustainable investment beliefs form your personal philosophy. This could be broken down into your mission, your vision and your values.

If this sounds too abstract, some people like to think in terms of asking themselves what role a business plays in society. Our sustainable investment beliefs help determine the kind of businesses that we want to support as investors. And they guide us towards companies that understand their role in society.

For example, I believe that all companies should be proactively thinking about their environmental footprint and have a clearly defined action plan for reducing any negative externalities caused. I use this belief in what I call 'corporate environmental proactivity' as a guiding principle for much of my own investment decision-making.

This means I actively seek out information on what certain companies are doing to reduce their footprint as well as looking for green and environmental-themed funds. It also helps me figure out the companies and sectors I definitely want to avoid – those that are doing significant environmental harm.

## Set your boundaries

Once you have articulated your beliefs, the next step is to consider and set your personal boundaries. What does this mean? Establish how much you are willing to do in terms of changes to your financial decision-making and investment choices.

To get there, ask yourself these kinds of questions:

- How important is it to me to become a sustainable investor? How much time do I want to put into this?

- Am I satisfied with a 'causing no harm' mantra, or do I want to target specific causes doing good?

- To what extent do I want external advice or input?

- To what extent is the impact of my investment important to me? Are there sacrifices I am willing to make?

- How much of my wealth do I want to allocate to sustainable investing? All or part?

- Am I willing to accept a lower financial return to achieve certain non-financial goals or specific social and environmental outcomes?

Being comfortable with how active a sustainable investor you want to be is key to your success. Remember, there is no right or wrong answer here. Your responses to the questions reflect your own motivation and appetite for change. Some people also like to think about this in terms of their personal 'risk appetite' – in other words, how much risk do you want to take in each decision and where do you draw the line?

This also involves understanding both the different risks associated with different types of investing and understanding your risk tolerance for these. For example, angel investing is considered relatively high risk because you are investing in early-stage companies, many without proven track records or revenue streams. Angel investing also sometimes requires investors to get intimately involved in the running of the investee companies – if you do not have time for this level of involvement, perhaps you need to think again.

## GET MORE EDUCATED, GET MORE EMPOWERED

I want to keep saying this out loud and clear... get educated and get empowered. There is a wealth of information and analysis out there so use it to your advantage.

If you are worried that you don't have the time, start small by aiming to set aside one hour a week to research the field. Bear in mind that you don't need to rush in. Take time to learn more about the issues that you care about so that you can make more informed decisions.

## How can I do this?

There are many ways you can learn more – here are some initial ideas:

- Sign up to newsletters and information from the organisations that work on the issues and priorities that you have identified as being important to you. For example, if you are concerned about environmental issues, check out CDP, which describes itself as a 'not-for-profit charity that runs the global disclosure system for investors, companies, cities, states and regions to manage their environmental impacts'.

- Connect with your local sustainable investment organisation – there is one in most regions as well as many at the national level. Keep an eye out for events and campaigns run by them, such as Good Money Week from UKSIF, which are specifically aimed at retail investors.

- Check out what is happening on the international scene as well – from the UN Global Compact to the Principles for Responsible Investment. These organisations may focus primarily on large institutional investors but some of their research and content is cutting-edge and can be useful to us as well.

- The GIIN (Global Impact Investing Network) is also one of the world's leading sources of data and perspectives on impact investing. Its Research Centre has a wealth of information including investor spotlights and profiles, GIIN-authored research and reports from other field-building organisations.

- Get active in online forums so you can learn about what others are thinking and doing. We see more and more of these pop up, especially those aimed at supporting women to invest more and to take control of their finances. If there is no specific content about sustainable investing, contact the forum administrators directly and suggest it.

- Hear what the experts have to say through reading blogs, attending events and lectures, watching TEDx Talks and YouTube videos. There is so much good content out there. (Perhaps a word of caution would be to avoid some of the old-school financial advice and investment blogs – this is probably not where you are going to get the kind of information you are looking for.)

## AUDIT YOURSELF, AND GET OTHERS TO DO THE SAME

Part of getting more empowered is also understanding where you currently stand. Ask yourself the big questions like... do I actually know where I am currently invested? Do I have a sense of whether or not these investments are in line with what I actually want for the future?

The reality is that many of us sign up to a retirement

pension or a savings plan and tick the 'ethical fund' or 'green investment plan' option. We feel momentarily better but often have absolutely no idea where these funds are actually going. I am the first one to admit that I have made this mistake, as I mentioned earlier.

However, it can sometimes turn out that these options are not so green, not so ethical. So it is time to go through the paperwork and make sure you really understand what you are currently investing in. Take a look at each investment (whether this is a pension plan or a savings product).[2] If your money is invested in listed companies (either directly or through a fund), check out their corporate sustainability reports which should be available on their websites.

Auditing yourself shouldn't be a one-off event. Be savvy and aim to do this on a regular basis, say once a year. And here's the other powerful action you can take – encourage others to do the same. If someone says to you, 'Oh, I am already invested in the green fund through my corporate pension plan', ask them what the main holdings of the fund are. Chances are you might be surprised – and so might they!

## How does regulation affect your pension?

In some countries pension regulation is becoming increasingly supportive of sustainable investing. For example, changes to UK pension regulation are meaning that most trust-based schemes will have to start disclosing their ESG policies – and this will include disclosure on climate change. In Europe, some aspects of the Sustainable Finance Action Plan are supporting enhanced ESG disclosure.

All of these trends will hopefully mean that demand for fund managers and advisors who are on board with sustainable investing will grow. It will also mean more investment products coming online that consider ESG factors.

## UNDERSTANDING WHAT COMPANIES ARE UP TO

Being a sustainable investor is about using our voice to push for higher environmental and social standards by the corporate sector. Of course, we can do this as consumers, but our investor voice can be equally powerful. To be effective in this role, we can look for the sustainability leaders and sustainability laggards, companies that are really making a difference or companies that continue to do harm despite weakening social licence to do so.

There are different sources of information and tools on corporate sustainability performance, such as the following:

### Company reports

Most big businesses now outline what they are doing to meet their Corporate Social Responsibility goals in their annual reports and/or on their website. Sometimes these are called Sustainability Reports.

What are you looking for when you read company disclosures?

- Read through relevant reports and website sections to understand the company's philosophy and whether its sustainability strategy makes sense to you.

- Ask yourself, does the company think about some of the priorities that I have identified as important to me?

- What kind of data does the company provide in these reports and does it reflect the commitments it makes?

- What are the company's plans for the future? Is it aiming high or pursuing a business-as-usual model?

- How does the company define success, if at all? What performance indicators or indicators of success does it use and do these improve over time?

- What is the CEO saying about sustainability, if anything?

### Leveraging non-profit organisations

Part of your due diligence should include taking a look at some of the amazing non-profit organisations that make it their job to keep an eye on the practices of companies. I firmly believe that the work of these organisations in holding companies to account forms a critical part of the ecosystem, so leverage their work and share their findings more broadly if you can.

Here are a few examples – take a look at their websites, read their research, follow their campaigns:

- BankTrack – the international tracking, campaigning and NGO support organisation focused on banks and the activities they finance.

- Business and Human Rights Resource Centre – an organisation dedicated to advancing human rights in business and eradicating abuse.

- CERES – a US-based organisation promoting sustainable business practices and solutions by working with companies and investors.

Also keep an eye out for B Corp – a private certification issued to for-profit companies by B Lab, a non-profit organisation with offices around the world. To be granted the certification, a company is legally required to consider the impact of its decisions on its workers, customers, suppliers, the community and the environment. The idea is to drive a new kind of business that balances purpose with profit.

## CEO commitments

Recently we've seen a number of leading CEOs come out and make big promises on sustainability and corporate responsibility. It is worth being aware of these, especially if you are looking at a specific company – check out what the CEO says and if any formal commitments have been made.

An interesting example is the Statement on the Purpose of a Corporation, released by the US-based Business Roundtable in 2019.[3] This was signed by 181 CEOs of major businesses, making a commitment to lead their companies for the benefit of all stakeholders – customers, employees, suppliers and shareholders. The idea is that CEOs have a responsibility beyond simply delivering value to shareholders, promoting the concept that businesses should be playing a role in improving society. It is an intriguing sign of the times that this is now on the table.

## PULLING IT ALL TOGETHER – YOUR SUSTAINABLE INVESTMENT STRATEGY

If you have followed the advice above, you will have done a lot of the groundwork but now it is time to start thinking strategically. This involves pulling together your thinking to design a plan of attack. The idea is that you put pen to paper and create a simple sustainable investment strategy, which can then be used to inform your choices, guide your investment decisions and take the next steps. Traditional institutional investors have an investment policy. Think of this as YOUR investment policy.

Don't panic – this doesn't have to be long and complicated, nor does it have to be set in stone. In fact, it is probably something you will want to revisit every year or so and will evolve, of course, as you travel through life.

**When you are ready, take the following steps:**

*Step 1: Review*
Look back at your sustainable investment beliefs and

reflect on what you have learned from your research and others you have spoken to, including experts as well as friends and family.

Developing your investment strategy to suit your situation is an essential factor. It's an opportunity to personalise your portfolio. This requires you taking into account your personal objectives but also your temperament and the time you can commit to managing it all.

## Step 2: Goal setting

Now it is time to identify your goals and write them down. What do you want your investments to accomplish? The more specific you are, the easier it will be to identify how and where you want to invest, and the more likely you are to use your investments to support your vision for the world.

*My goal is to... for example:*

- Not invest in companies in the fossil fuel sector.

- Identify companies with sustainable sourcing strategies.

- Directly invest in clean energy companies.

- Consider investing in companies that are committed to racial equity.

## Step 3: Acting on your personal audit

As we've said, if you have existing investments, make sure you know what you are in. This includes any pension schemes you may be a member of, as well as mutual funds, stocks, bonds or other investments you already hold. Take this analysis and make the changes you need to.

*Step 4: Measuring success*
Think about how you will measure success, your personal success. It's not an easy task to measure impact but it's worth having some sense of what success would look like for you. This is why I use the SDGs, because under each SDG there are targets and KPIs. I find these really useful to help me think about measuring my own success.

*Step 5: Action planning*
And finally, start planning out the actions you need to take to move you from A to B:
  *I will… for example:*

- Change the allocation in my current pension plan to a different fund that is aligned with my values (e.g. a green fund).

- Speak with my pension plan provider about alternative fund options or new funds that may become available in the future that are more closely aligned with my sustainable investment beliefs.

- Follow up with my financial advisor on new investment products that might be of interest.

- Speak with my bank about what sustainable investment products it offers.

Being a sustainable investor is about making well-informed, well-considered decisions. Not just taking longer to make decisions but making decisions for the longer term. Use your well-thought-out strategy to build your confidence as a sustainable investor.

Research also indicates that women are more likely to confer with their peers when making decisions. So, discuss your plan with your friends and family. Get their feedback.

## DON'T STOP HERE

### Talk to your financial advisor

I've said it before, but I am going to reiterate it. It is essential that you engage with a financial planner or financial advisor as you work all of this out. Why? Because the setting of goals and strategy should also be completed in alignment with your broader financial goals (how much money you need when and so on). Speaking directly with an investment professional should help ensure that you cover this.

### Keep in mind

It is easy to get attached to your money! Investments do go up and down and investment prices constantly change. Drops in the value of your portfolio are normal so try not to panic. As long as you are doing your homework, investing intelligently and consciously, keep your cool and look to the long term.

## Urge family and friends to take action

When discussions with friends and family come up, engage with them too. How to do this?

- Share interesting articles and experiences.

- Talk openly about your sustainable investment beliefs – many women have not thought about this approach as an option so sharing your personal experience with friends can be a powerful opener.

- Use your social media avenues to share examples of what you are invested in. The more we talk openly about what makes a good company the better.

## Put pressure on the financial industry to take action

We also need to engage with the financial industry, through conversations with our banks and financial advisors. We want them to change too.

We need to counter any industry bias that does not fully listen to the needs of women. But at the same time, we need to demonstrate that there is demand for sustainable investment products.

Speak directly with your bank or financial advisor to let them know what you want. Contact your pension plan provider and ask questions. The more they hear the message, the more likely they are to take action. Keep an eye out for campaigns you may want to get behind. For example, in the UK, Richard Curtis (of *Four Weddings and a Funeral* and *Bridget Jones's Diary* fame) has co-founded the Make My Money Matter campaign, calling for pension funds to be 'invested in building a future we can be proud of, economies we can rely on, and an environment we can thrive in'.[4]

## Stay active yourself

Becoming a sustainable investor isn't a one-off event. It is an active choice that probably needs some regular circling back. So, keep actively engaged and keep going back over these steps, setting a regular time to do this.

It is likely that your investment beliefs may shift as the world around us changes. Set aside time to review your priorities regularly, and also check in with those around you.

## Join a sustainable investing community, be part of the movement

We've already spoken about some of the local and regional sustainable investment organisations, some of which include information and events for individual investors. As well as these, seek out if there are any other sustainable investing communities, and if you can't find one, maybe set one up? Like old-school investment clubs but with a difference!

There are an increasing number of female-focused investing initiatives offering both online and in-person support. While not explicitly focused on sustainable investing, these do target women and their financial health, and sometimes include sustainable investing as a particular theme. For example, take a look at:

- SmartPurse – an interactive knowledge and networking platform for women to learn all about money and discuss and plan money matters. The website includes a 16-module interactive financial learning path with checklists, templates and personal guidance aimed at simplifying how to get financially fit. SmartPurse also hosts events and meet-ups and provides access to financial coaches for women.

- The New Savvy – a financial, investments and career platform for women in Asia, offering events, resources and 101 guides to support women in becoming savvier with their money. The New Savvy advocates greater awareness and healthier financial habits for women, using high-quality content and working through education, media and conferences.

- Ladies Finance Club – for women in Australia who want to take control of their financial futures and get money savvy. Offering events, courses, blogs and other beneficial resources, the website is an excellent place to start.

For sustainable and impact investing content in particular, the following offer content for female investors:

- Moxie Future – an education, community and blog platform that I set up a few years ago for women who want to learn more about sustainable investing and the issues relevant to its universe. Our aim is to really engage with women about what we can do with our money and stimulate conversations. With global coverage, the website includes a wealth of information from getting started to research on female investment preferences and sustainability. We have a fantastic group of people involved – with an Advisory Committee of leading global voices and Ambassadors who support our outreach.

- Invest for Better – a US-based non-profit campaign with a mission to help women demystify impact investing, take control of their capital and mobilise their money for good. The website provides a whole host of resources, tips on getting started and stories from other female investors. In particular, check out the Invest for Better Circles – a growing national network of small, peer-to-peer learning and activation groups. The Toolkit offers guidance for circle leaders – individuals who want to build small communities of women committed to increasing their personal knowledge and participation in values-aligned and impact investing.

## ELLEN REMMER, CHAMPION, INVEST FOR BETTER

*Invest for Better is a nonprofit campaign on a mission to help women demystify impact investing, take control of their capital and mobilise their money for good.*

### Why does sustainable investing present such an exciting opportunity for women?

While women have played a powerful role in philanthropy, they have been grossly underrepresented in the professional investing world and among primary household investors. Impact investing appeals to women because it brings purpose and the possibility of social change to the art of investing. I'm so excited to see women engaging with their investments now as it means women will shape the future of the New Economy.

### What is your advice for women just getting started?

The most important first steps are to ask a lot of questions – of yourself, your advisors or anybody connected with your investments. How is your money currently invested and why? What exactly do you own in your portfolio? How do those holdings match your personal values? What are the other investing options that would match your values? What are the implications of moving your money?

### How can women support one another on their sustainable investing journey?

If women can come together into trusted communities of support and accountability, we will start to see their money move into impact in a material way. Invest for Better Circles are one approach, but it can happen in all kinds of contexts.

## EIGHT

## IT IS NOT PLAIN SAILING

By now, I trust you are thinking to yourself: 'This all makes perfect sense.' If that is the case then you are likely also thinking: 'Why isn't every woman doing this?'

I know from bitter experience, as I have grappled with my own investment decisions over the last few years, that attempting to go full throttle with sustainable investing choices isn't all plain sailing. Exploring the reasons why this isn't easy matters. Because once we explore, we can then see that these reasons are not insurmountable. They simply require some thinking through and making certain leaps of faith, much like any other form of investment.

We know that women are held back by a few complex issues when it comes to traditional investing. So, we have to assume that these issues are even more pronounced when we talk about sustainable investing. The lack of confidence many women feel around money and investment is accentuated when talking about linking investment decisions to values and impact.

But if you are reading this book, you have already taken the first critical step. Let's now consider how understanding the barriers we face can help us towards solving and overcoming them.

## IT'S STILL A NASCENT INDUSTRY

The last couple of years have really seen the sustainable investment industry develop but it is still a long way off being considered mainstream. In the institutional investor world, there have certainly been some significant developments, especially when it comes to putting in place formal ESG policies, frameworks and reporting. However, in the retail investor world – the world where you and I live – progress has been much slower. In fact, at times, non-existent.

Why is this the case? As always, it can be attributed to multiple complex and interconnected reasons. In the following section we touch on some of these as well as consider potential solutions or realistic next steps.

### Lack of standard or common definition
The lack of a standard definition still seems to be a sticking point, as the collective 'we' continues to quibble over what sustainable investing means. This seems to hold some people back as they are not entirely sure how to grasp the concept and therefore use this as a reason not to take concrete action.

**Solution?** The first step is to stop getting so hung up about the definition. Accept that sustainable investment in its purest form is about achieving positive change in an area or on an issue which the investor is passionate about. These areas invariably have a social and/or environmental dimension. Of course, then the detailed strategy varies from one person to another as there is no 'one-size-fits-all'. But that's OK because we are all headed in the same direction.

## Limited options available to retail investors

Financial product providers are moving slowly in terms of providing suitable and accessible investment products to make it easy for us to invest sustainably. This continues to exacerbate the problem that sustainable investing remains fairly undemocratic – i.e. only for those with stacks of cash and private bankers willing to help them (and charge the fees).

For the ordinary woman options continue to remain quite limited. Furthermore, it can also depend on where you live – for example, if you live in Europe, it is likely that you will come across a few sustainable investment products. At the same time, in European markets you should find it reasonably easy to find sustainability information on both companies and funds. This may not be the case in other markets.

**Solution?** It is clear there is a need for more innovative, scalable products to cater to us as retail investors. So, we need to start asking for them. Really. Go to our banks, to our advisors, to anyone that will listen and tell them it's not good enough to say that doing good with our money is not possible. Some are already beginning to, so it can be done. Let's drive demand and make it clear that sustainable investing is the future of investing.

## Getting the right kind of advice

Many financial advisors are not familiar with sustainable investing and often banks are not much better. What's worse is that there seems to be a disconnect between what advisors believe their clients want and the actual needs of investors looking to get stuck into sustainable investing. The end result is that many female investors feel they are not being heard by qualified investment professionals. This is a critical piece of the jigsaw, so we need to figure it out.

**Solution?** Without a doubt, more education of financial advisors is needed. As financial market regulators become savvier on sustainable investing, I suspect we will see expectations rise and in fact this is already starting to happen in some countries. For our part, we must not take no for an answer. Chapter 11 is dedicated to the topic of working with financial advisors – how to find the right advisor for you and how to get the most out of the relationship, particularly when it comes to sustainable investing.

## Quality of data

As with any emerging industry, a lot of work needs to be done to support its development and to grow it through to maturity. This is undoubtedly the case with sustainable investing, particularly when it comes to the quality of data available. The investment industry needs both transparent processes and good-quality data on a company's performance in order to do its job effectively.

When it comes to sustainable investing, the primary data is based on environmental, social and governance criteria. We have made a lot of progress on ESG data but it is still a work in progress. Financial markets around the world have been plugging away at guidelines and regulations, in particular on corporate disclosure requirements. Some companies have made tremendous advances, others are seriously lagging. Improving transparency and disclosure is necessary for us to move forward towards improved data from which to make more informed decisions.

**Solution?** Unfortunately, there is not too much we, as individual investors, can do at this stage. A great deal of work is under way, and we must keep a watching brief. As an investor, be aware that the lack of standardisation and wide-ranging nature of ESG ratings and data sets can be overwhelming. In part it is about the quality of data, but it is also about the level of transparency, which can be a cultural issue, at a market or company level.

### Higher costs
Yes, historically fees have been higher for sustainable investment products. This has primarily been because more work is entailed for the fund manager. The good

news is that fees have come down quite dramatically for sustainable investment products. Given that it is a lot easier to find out what different companies are doing now (e.g. in company annual reports and the extensive work that some investment research houses are doing), the workload has really been reduced making it less costly all round.

**Solution?** Remember that the more people choose sustainable investments, the more costs will come down, so, again, we play a role as drivers of demand. Costs are also being helped by technical advances and as this progresses so too do the number of accessible investment products for investors like us. Chapter 12 explores the influence of technology in greater depth.

## Measuring outcomes and impact
Measuring outcomes and impact is critical.

Any investment has an impact on the real world. Period. Whether, for example, it be the environmental footprint of a project or asset; the number of jobs created; or the impact on the local economy. However, these impacts can often be entirely opaque to the investor. In part, this is due to lack of information and data provided in a consistent and standardised form.

We know that much has been achieved in a short space of time, but the field of sustainable investing will not go mainstream until we have a robust evidence base to credibly establish the ability to deliver positive social and environmental outcomes alongside financial returns. Certainly, it is not an easy issue to contend with, particularly for an individual investor.

**Solution?** We cannot ignore the challenge of measuring the outcomes of our investment decisions. And we should certainly not avoid it simply because it is challenging. Good work is being done, and we can be part of it.

For regular investors like you and me, without private bankers to shape our portfolios or sufficient assets to engage a specialised wealth manager, we have to do our best to define and track the positive impacts we can have. Much more needs to be done, but here are some ideas to get you started.

*Revisit the SDGs and their individual targets*

Once again, I recommend you go back to the SDGs and the 169 targets that sit beneath them. You may not be able to set specific KPIs at this stage but the SDG framework can help you hone your thinking on desired outcomes and impacts. Talking the language of the SDGs is helpful because, as we highlighted before, some wealth managers are developing frameworks around them. It is worth looking at what they are doing in terms of reporting to their clients on SDG impact.

The Cambridge Institute for Sustainability Leadership has also launched 'The Investment Impact Framework', based on a set of six open-source metrics which investors can use as proxies for measuring their progress towards particular SDGs.[1] Take a look.

*Engage with financial services providers*

Assuming you are planning to have some form of conversation with your bank or financial advisor, raise the impact topic at the outset of this chat. Be clear about how you feel about impact and the kind of metrics you think are useful when measuring this. In particular, you can ask about this at the investment fund level. Some of the metrics might include:

- Carbon footprint – how much $CO_2$ the companies in an investment portfolio are emitting.

- Water and waste – similar to carbon, measuring the water and waste footprints of companies in an investment portfolio.

- Social impact – for example, the number of people whose quality of life has improved because of certain products or company performance in terms of diversity, or position on racial justice issues.

- Engagement – how active fund managers are in engaging with companies to encourage them to improve their impact on society (although this can be extra challenging to put metrics around).

*Check out some of the measurement tools*

There are some cool tools out there that can be quite illuminating and certainly help you think further about the outcomes you want to achieve. Here are a few examples:

- **IRIS+** Operated by the Global Impact Investment Network, IRIS+ is a rating system that aims to translate impact investing goals – such as gender equity, climate change and affordable housing – into results.[2] The tool is designed with the investor in mind. It shows metrics of measurability that a business will be expected to produce in order to win the confidence of an investor. The good news is that it is a free, publicly available resource.

- **Global Impact Investment Rating System (GIIRS)** Created over a decade ago, and originally intended to apply sustainability criteria to private investments made through venture capital and private equity funds, GIIRS was the brainchild of the B Lab (the non-profit organisation that administers B Corp certification).[3] It is a system for assessing the social and environmental impact of developed and emerging market companies and funds with a transparency ratings and analytics approach.

- **Sustainability Accounting Standards Board (SASB)** The Sustainability Accounting Standards Board is a non-profit that was established in 2011 to develop sustainability accounting standards. These include industry-specific standards and various tools such as Navigator, which analyses 77 different industries along a consistent range of environmental, social and governance metrics.[4] Unfortunately, it is not free but there is a wealth of information on the SASB website, and looking at the metrics it uses for specific industries could help formulate your own decision-making.

## FINAL FOOD FOR THOUGHT

The sustainable investing movement is growing, and we need now to embrace measurement, data and transparency fully. As the movement gets bigger, we must develop the data and evidence to underpin the compelling narratives on what can be achieved.

Standards will help to build investor confidence. To deliver social and environmental returns at the same time as financial returns *is* possible and we need to continue to develop the tools to understand and track this. In particular, investors, entrepreneurs and analysts require accessible and reliable data that demonstrates the breadth of the field, including the return and impact spectrum offered.

It can be frustrating thinking about outcome and impact, and putting tangible metrics in place to understand what you have done and over what time frame. Don't let that frustration hold you back. I strongly encourage you to pick a metric (or more than one) and just get on with it! You can find some way to track your investment portfolio. And measurement will only improve as more investors enter the space. You are changing the world, hang in there.

# NINE

## IT CAN BE DONE – HERE'S HOW

In this chapter I want to bring to life how all this can be done, taking some example 'issues' and running through how you might want to think about them and reflect them in your own investment portfolio.

First, we do a deep dive into climate change – what it means to us as investors and the kind of actions we could take. Then we look at the world of fashion – an industry where the issue of sustainability is becoming hotter than the latest fashion trend. At this point you might be asking, given that this is a book targeting women, why are we not looking at diversity and gender from a sustainable investing perspective? Don't worry – we devote Chapter 10 to a discussion on the important topic of gender-lens investing.

# CLIMATE CHANGE

## The issue

There is now clear and strong scientific consensus around the causes and impacts of climate change. It is our responsibility. It is having devastating effects and we need to be moving much faster than we are. The Paris Agreement, agreed in 2015, set the long-term goal of keeping the increase in the global average temperature to well below 2 degrees Celsius above pre-industrial levels, and actually to pursue efforts to limit this temperature increase even further to 1.5 degrees Celsius.[1]

Fantastic commitment. However, this was followed by bad news in 2018 from the world's leading climate scientists – authors of the landmark report by the UN Intergovernmental Panel on Climate Change.[2] They warned us that there was in fact only a small window of opportunity to keep global warming to a maximum of 1.5 degrees Celsius. In 2018 that window was estimated as being 12 years.

At this point, even half a degree will significantly worsen the risk of extreme heat, massive floods and calamitous droughts. The physical impacts and the resulting poverty will affect hundreds of millions of people.[3] To avoid this, which is looking increasingly challenging, we need urgent change. This change needs to occur in our economies, societies, local communities, financial markets. All of which is highly ambitious but is potentially feasible if we act boldly today.

Since the Paris Agreement, the topics of climate risk and climate resilience have moved centre stage, dominating debate across national governments and intergovernmental bodies, within civil society and in the media. Climate change, and the resultant discussion on how to deal with it, is having an impact across all industries, sectors and areas of our lives.

## Climate change translated in the financial world

In the financial industry, no market, no financial institutions, no investor is immune to the influence and effect that climate change is having. We can no longer talk of whether it will happen, rather when. Climate change is truly a disruptive force – and this presents different considerations for investors like us.

## Companies should have plans in place

Most companies – certainly listed ones – are now aware of the enormous impact of climate change on their business models, and so are building climate risk into their strategic planning process. From an investor perspective, look out for what companies are doing on climate change, in particular whether they are putting in place climate resilience plans. If climate does not feature in any corporate documents, be concerned. And of course, this is particularly important for companies in sectors directly impacted such as energy, natural resources, infrastructure, motor vehicles and so on. You would expect these companies to be ahead of the game if they are managing climate risk effectively.

## Have you heard about stranded assets?

Stranded assets are essentially assets that end up having to be unexpectedly devalued or suffer a write-down (the accounting term used to describe the fall in book value of something). Sometimes, in worst case scenarios, these assets can also be converted into a liability on the books. This devaluation is unexpected, unplanned for or premature, so it is a big issue for the financial health of any company facing such risks.

Why does this happen? For a variety of reasons. Carbon Tracker is a UK-based organisation that was at the centre of developing the concept of stranded assets. It did so 'to get people thinking about the implications of not adjusting investment in line with the emissions trajectories required to limit global warming.'[4] Carbon Tracker explains the different potential reasons behind the stranding of assets:

1. Regulatory stranding – this occurs due to a change in policy or legislation.
2. Economic stranding – when a change in relative costs/prices occurs.
3. Physical stranding – caused due to physical events such as distance/flood/drought.

Let's put this into the real world starting with our energy sector. The relevance of stranded assets to the fossil fuel industry is vast – and really where it all began. As the world moves towards fossil fuel phase-out, which we know it must do, given the commitments made under the Paris Agreement, coal and other fossil fuel reserves are likely to become 'stranded', i.e. of reduced financial value. As we transition to a low-carbon economy, these reserves (assets) will not come out of the ground. Fossil fuel companies may be recognising these currently as financially valuable, but the reality is that, in our carbon-constrained world, they will no longer be able to earn an economic return. They are stranded in the ground.

This matters to investors because it represents a substantial potential risk on the company's balance sheet. The International Energy Agency has warned that $1.3 trillion of oil and gas assets could be left stranded by 2050, if the fossil fuel industry does not adapt to greener climate policies.[5] So if you are keen to be an energy investor, you will want to be ahead of the anti-carbon curve. You now know enough not to be taken in by old-school 'wisdom' on this. The fossil fuel companies of today may not look as attractive an investment in our low-carbon future.

### Watch consumer sentiment

It is glaringly apparent that consumer sentiment is shifting, particularly for younger generations. People are becoming more aware of the environmental impact that their consumption patterns are having as well as the need to radically address the root causes of climate change. An excellent example of how this changing consumer sentiment has fed through into our thoughts on money is the DivestInvest global campaign – a campaign that challenges the social licence of fossil fuel companies to operate as they currently do, while making it possible for renewable industries to thrive. The campaign has been relentlessly encouraging investors to move quickly out of fossil fuels and into sustainable and clean energy investments. We have seen this take hold in several countries. With the intergenerational transfer of wealth happening, many millennials are seeking to invest that wealth with purpose, and climate change is featuring high on their priority list.

## It's not all downside risks

In order for our economies to become future-fit, we need to radically transform the way we work, the way we consume, the way we live. The interesting companies to watch will be those that are deploying capital to take advantage of the investment opportunities that climate change brings. For example, if you think about the motor industry, take a look at the big financial bets companies are making on the future of electric cars.

## The role of technology

It is stating the obvious that technology is vitally important because new markets and investment opportunities will likely emerge as climate resilience technology becomes available. There are multiple areas where green tech can play a considerable role – from the use of remote sensors in agriculture to renewable storage solutions; from smart grids supporting the distribution of renewable power generation to the use of drones in conservation efforts.

Today we are seeing a new wave of investment targeting cutting-edge technological solutions to climate change. You as an investor can avoid certain companies and sectors – such as fossil fuels – but you can also use climate change as a form of positive screening, actively choosing to invest in green tech companies that are addressing climate change.

## Sustainable investors, what can we do?

Climate change is not going away. Al Gore posited recently in the *New York Times*:

> Now we need to ask ourselves: Are we really helpless and unwilling to respond to the gravest threat faced by civilization? Is it time, as some have begun to counsel, to despair, surrender and focus on 'adapting' to the progressive loss of the conditions that have supported the flourishing of humanity? Are we really moral cowards, easily manipulated into lethargic complacency by the huge continuing effort to deceive us into ignoring what we see with our own eyes?[6]

He has a point. There are many different ways in which we can take action, but it is often overlooked that our money matters too. If climate change is a concern to you and you are wondering how you can redirect your investments, a useful starting resource is the US SIF publication *Investing to Curb Climate Change: A Guide for the Individual*

*Investor.*[7] Have a read and start thinking about your investment decisions in the following ways:

## Reducing risk

Our first point of leverage is to reduce the risk in our investment portfolio – this basically means avoiding our exposure to companies that are less likely to do well in a climate-stressed world. We've talked a lot about fossil fuel companies and I highly recommend checking out the amazing work of As You Sow, a US-based non-profit.[8]

As You Sow produces a wealth of information, research and reports that can support you in understanding more about climate change from an investor perspective and how to get out of fossil fuels. In particular, check out Fossil Free Funds – a search platform and database of the thousands of open-end and exchange-traded mutual funds, built to help people understand whether their money is being used to extract and consume fossil fuels.[9] Note that it is currently for US investors only, covering mutual funds and ETFs, not company-level data, rather this is aggregated for the 3,000 most held funds. With more demand and more resources hopefully the Fossil Free Funds tool can be expanded, and it is definitely worth a look, and supporting if you can. As You Sow also has other tools, including extending the climate impact of investing to Deforestation Free Funds which now cover resources such as palm oil, timber and beef.

Don't forget, it's not just fossil fuels to be aware of. Other carbon-intensive industries such as steel, chemicals and engineering are likely to be impacted by new and emerging climate regulations. Keep it in mind that you need to ensure that your portfolio does not run the risk of stranded assets and that this risk can sit across several industries.

## Identifying opportunities

The second point of leverage is to look for companies and funds that will benefit from the transition to a low-carbon economy. As has been a common theme throughout the book, do your research. We've talked before about a company's sustainability report as an excellent starting point. Find out how transparent companies are on their climate change strategies. You are looking for companies that disclose information on their internal climate policies and this includes plans to transition to a low-carbon operating environment.

Climate disclosures are getting much better and this is largely due to the work of the Task Force on Climate-related Financial Disclosures (TCFD).[10] The TCFD was set up by the Financial Stability Board to develop a set of recommendations for voluntary and consistent climate-related financial risk disclosures by companies. Admittedly, it has been a long journey for the task force, but the effect that its recommendations have had on the enhanced level of information about the nature and the size of climate risk is important.

More and more tools are coming online for retail investors to make it easier to get behind the low-carbon boom. For example, US SIF hosts a public tool for individual investors to 'compare cost, financial performance, screens and voting records of competing funds'.[11] It is a useful tool to identify funds in the climate and clean tech space.

There are more and more equity and bond mutual funds and ETFs that have been created with the low-carbon transition in mind – for example, Legal & General Investment Management has launched a unit trust version of its Future World index tracker fund for retail investors. We have also seen a boom in the number of green bond funds available.

If climate change is a big issue for you and you want to focus on it as an investment theme for your own portfolio, start by doing your own research and then work with your financial advisor to help identify opportunities for more climate-focused investments.

## Using your voice

Again, another theme of the book – with climate change becoming such an urgent issue, use your investor voice. We haven't talked about it much, but shareholder engagement (shareholders communicating their views, concerns and opinions to a company's board of directors) is also something worth considering.

Fiona Reynolds, Chief Executive for the Principles for Responsible Investment, highlights this:

Retail investors should not underestimate – or fail to use – the power they wield through voting rights.

This is a great way for investors to make their voices heard on a number of corporate initiatives, including climate resolutions.

In recent years, we have seen an unprecedented number of climate-related resolutions at major oil and gas companies as well as companies in related sectors.[12]

It's not just your own investment accounts through which you can use your voice. You may also be able to influence the investment decisions of the organisations you are connected to such as university endowments, local government operating funds, pension funds and religious institutions.

## Final thought

Being a climate change investor is going to get easier, in part because regulators are putting pressure on companies and financial institutions to be more transparent about their climate risks and actions. For example, Mark Carney, the former Governor of the Bank of England, has been very vocal on pushing industries to do more. He has warned major businesses that they have limited time to agree to rules for reporting climate risks. If they don't then global regulators will devise their own rules and make them compulsory.[13]

It is also worth reflecting on what we have learned from the COVID-19 pandemic because climate impact events are similarly unpredictable in terms of when they will occur. Droughts, crop failures, floods, storms and heatwaves could create shocks similar to COVID-19 – sudden and experienced dramatically on a localised level, bringing not only a health crisis but also a market crisis. This tells us we need to be better prepared and we need to be investing in the right things. Today.

## SUSTAINABLE FASHION

### The issue
The fashion industry is a real powerhouse for global development. It is one of the world's largest consumer industries – worth an estimated value of $3 trillion; representing 2 per cent of the world's Gross Domestic Product (GDP); and employing over 60 million people along its value chain.[14]

Its size is enormous and so too are the environmental and social issues associated with the industry. These issues are complex and wide-ranging – from putting pressure on extremely limited natural resources to protecting the rights of all those involved in the value chain.

### Some stats to make you sit up
Let us reflect on the reality of fashion's environmental and societal footprint:

- The fashion industry is responsible for 10 per cent of annual global carbon emissions, more than all international flights and maritime shipping combined.

Every year the fashion industry uses 93 billion cubic metres of water – enough to meet the consumption needs of 5 million people.[15]

- An estimated 246 million children are employed in child labour.[16] This is a real issue for the fashion industry because garment factories have often been in a 'race to the bottom' to provide cheap fashion and to provide it fast. The result has been many children involved all along the supply chain of the fashion industry.

- Health and safety issues are rife in the fashion industry. You may recall that in 2013, more than 1,100 people died in the Rana Plaza garment factory collapse in Bangladesh. Yet, despite such shocking events, safety issues continue to plague factories across the developing world and many claim that little has changed.

- More than $500 billion of value is lost every year due to clothing underutilisation and the lack of recycling. Wastage in the industry is unfathomable, the fashion industry is the second-largest polluter in the world; 5.2 per cent of waste in our landfills is textiles and 23 kilos of GHGs are generated for each kilo of fabric produced.[17]

## What's going on with fashion's sustainability?

The harsh reality is that we are buying more and wearing for less time. In the 15 years from 2000 to 2015, clothing production almost doubled.[18] To over 100 billion units per year!

Why is this? There are a number of reasons but it is primarily driven by the growing middle-class population across the world, compounded by the 'fast fashion' phenomenon seen in mature economies, whereby clothes are offered at lower prices, with quicker turnaround of new styles and more collections produced each year.

At the same time, there are some tremendous issues that the industry is grappling with. For example, recently Burberry admitted destroying $37 million in unsold clothes, accessories and perfume instead of selling it off cheaply – taking the total value of goods it has destroyed over the past five years to more than $117 million.[19] Why? In order to protect the brand's perceived exclusivity and value.

And it's not just high-end brands; fast fashion is also at it. In 2017, H&M reportedly burned about 19 tonnes of obsolete clothing (the equivalent of 50,000 pairs of jeans) in a waste-to-energy facility run by one of Sweden's energy giants – meanwhile making a lot of noise about its in-store recycling points and so-called Conscious Collection.[20]

Over the last decade, a number of brands in the fashion industry have begun to do things differently. Pioneers like Stella McCartney, Raven + Lily, Akola Project, Reformation, Patagonia and Apolis are changing how clothes are made and how the industry works. These front-runners are coming up with innovative ways to protect our environment and to take care of the people who make their products.

**Does acting sustainably benefit the business of fashion?**
With such enormous challenges facing the industry and with so many opportunities to reduce the impact on planet and people, sustainable fashion is worth giving more thought to as an important and exciting sustainable investment trend.

What's more, taking action on sustainability not only improves the social and environmental performance of the industry, it seems that it also results in a strong business case for adding value. For example, Boston Consulting Group found that taking action on sustainability can raise the earnings before interest and taxes (EBIT) margin by 1 to 2 percentage points for apparel companies.[21] That's an encouraging increase.

As we look to the future, the fact that the number of fashion brands describing themselves as ethical or sustainable is on the rise shows that they also see that consumers are prioritising this. In turn, this tells us that it is not going away – the future of fashion must be sustainable. For investors, that's a big green light.

## Sustainable investors, what can we do?
As consumers, we know how we can begin to effect positive change in the fashion industry, quite simply through the purchasing decisions we make. But as investors – particularly those of us motivated to address environmental and social challenges through our investment decisions – the fashion industry is a harder nut to crack.

But we can make change happen and here are some ideas on how:

## Get fashion smart

There's a wealth of research out there, so it's easy to learn more about the environmental and social issues that plague this industry. Take a look at the *Pulse of the Fashion Industry*, a report published by the Global Fashion Agenda, in collaboration with Boston Consulting Group.[22] It's long but worth a read – assessing the industry's environmental and social performance, revealing where the industry stands and highlighting case studies of companies doing good stuff.

## Audit yourself

We have said it before but let's say it again – know what you are currently invested in. Chances are you may not know which fashion and apparel companies you are investing in, particularly if you are invested in mutual funds and ETFs. So take some time to run through the company holdings in those funds.

FashionUnited lists the 100 largest listed companies worldwide within the apparel and fashion industry – the FashionUnited Top 100 Index.[23] These top 100 companies (by market capitalisation) represent a market value of over $1 trillion. That's a big influencer on how we value our people and our planet.

While you may not be able to do a lot with your existing holdings, being aware is a critical first step. Use this to inform future investment decisions, particularly when looking at different investment funds you could move into. Recently, under the auspices of UN Climate Change, the Fashion Industry Charter for Climate Action was launched – with the vision of achieving net-zero emissions by 2050. It is interesting to see which companies have signed up to it and it can give you, the investor, some insight into what companies may be up to – or not.

## Push for transparency

We have already talked about how transparency matters – at the product level (e.g. information on how a product is sourced, its environmental footprint, etc.). Transparency also matters at the corporate level (e.g. the processes a company has in place to source sustainably, protect its employees, report to its stakeholders, etc.).

As investors, we should look for what information apparel companies provide – in particular, start with their sustainability reports. The more companies know these are being read, the more attention they will give to their contents. And if you think shareholders (however big or small) need more information then don't be shy – tell them!

## Is crowdfunding an option?

Crowdfunding – raising many small amounts of money from a large number of people, typically via an online platform – is a great option for supporting start-ups in the sustainable fashion field. Many crowdfunding platforms host campaigns for different types of early-stage fashion companies – such as Kickstarter's campaign for Sustain which makes 'all-natural clothing'.[24]

Rewards-based crowdfunding is also gaining traction in the fashion sector – for example, take a look at Next Chapter, a Hong Kong-based funding platform that focuses on securing investment for female entrepreneurs.[25] A good example is its campaign raising investment for Basics for Basics, which rewards investors with clothing from its ethical range.

## Keep your eyes open

If sustainable fashion is your thing, as an investor it is not always an obvious investment theme. Keep an eye out for new funds that may emerge in the future. For example, US-based Alante Capital is a venture capital fund 'backing innovative companies that radically improve social and environmental sustainability in the textile and apparel industry'.

### KARLA MORA, FOUNDER AND MANAGING PARTNER, ALANTE CAPITAL

*Alante Capital is a venture capital fund investing in innovative technologies that enable a resilient, sustainable future for apparel production and retail.*

**Why did you set up Alante Capital and why is sustainable fashion such an important investment theme?**

I set up Alante because I saw a huge opportunity for a systemic shift to occur within the apparel industry and wanted to be a part of shifting it towards sustainability. The way that clothing is made, worn and disposed of has created an enormous social and environmental problem.

Over the past decade, sustainable brands and forward-thinking consumers have begun driving demand for sustainable products across food, beauty and fashion.

At the same time, resource scarcity and climate risk were driving mainstream apparel brands to think about sustainability as a risk mitigator as well as a way to stand out to consumers in an ever-changing retail landscape. These mainstream apparel brands began to publicly make commitments towards sustainability, and innovative start-ups launched to answer the call and address huge market opportunities in apparel at the intersection of sustainability and profitability. What is needed now is capital to help these start-ups scale viable solutions that can replace negative incumbent business practices.

Investing to improve sustainability in the fashion industry is massively important to our collective effort to address our changing climate. But it is also the direction that this enormous industry is headed which creates a very compelling investment opportunity that will drive much-needed capital to this space.

**What kind of impact are you looking to achieve with Alante Capital?**

Transformative.

# PART III

PART III

# TEN

## SISTERS DOING IT FOR THEMSELVES – GENDER-SMART INVESTING

This book is FOR women. This chapter is ABOUT women. Because there is a really exciting investment trend emerging that sits well within the sustainable investing universe – that of gender-smart or gender-lens investing, which is the practice of investing for financial return while also considering the benefits to women, through improving economic opportunities and social well-being for girls and women.

Just to be clear at the outset, we are not talking about Microfinance. Microfinance is a type of banking service that targets individuals and small businesses that have no other access to conventional banking or funding opportunities. Because women often fall into this category, some people automatically assume that gender-smart investing is only about Microfinance. That is not the case – gender-smart investing is something different.

## GENDER-SMART INVESTING DEFINED

Its definition is broad, crossing multiple sectors and with different components. It is probably best defined by Catalyst at Large,[1] an organisation founded by Suzanne Biegel,[2] a global leader in gender-smart investing:

> Gender-smart investing integrates gender-based factors into investment strategy, process and analysis in order to improve business and financial outcomes, achieve a spectrum of risk-adjusted returns, achieve better social and environmental outcomes, and move towards gender equality. Employing strategies that recognise gender factors can help investors spot market opportunities where others might miss them, or identify risks more accurately, while simultaneously creating a more equitable world for everyone.

The concept of investing with a gender lens has been on the table for a few years now, and excitingly some progress is being made. No longer just about equality and rights, there is more and more recognition of the importance of gender diversity to corporate performance, risk management and board governance. At the same time, gender equality and women's rights are front and centre of everyone's mind, particularly in light of the #MeToo movement, the Women's March and other gender-related campaigns. These broader movements are having ripple effects across all industries, including the world of finance. Some investment firms are now creating investment products across different asset classes that seek to help women advance in economic terms, attempting to reflect gender issues – from the number of women represented in corporate boardrooms to how women are treated on factory floors.

## Tell me more

When we invest with a gender lens, we are following an investment thesis that is essentially seeking to turn the abstract concept of investing to benefit women into something tangible and actionable.

There are different aspects to being gender-smart in your investment decisions, resulting in different outcomes, all of which seek to deliver positive benefits to women and girls. Again referencing Catalyst at Large, gender-smart investing opportunities can be realised in the following ways:[3]

1. Improving women's access to capital by investing in businesses that are woman-led, co-founded or owned.
2. Investing in products and services that capture the women's market or help solve social issues that disproportionately impact women and girls.
3. Creating or investing in funds and structured investment vehicles with a strong approach to gender equity and diversity.
4. Using a gender lens to identify potential risks and opportunities across the value chain.

So, you can see that there are many different angles you can take as a gender-smart investor. You might be investing with the intention of addressing a specific gender issue or promoting gender equality, such as boardroom representation. Or you might be investing using a gender approach to inform your investment decisions, such as a particular process that focuses on gender, or strategy that looks at a company's mission to address gender issues.[4]

## WHY DOES IT MATTER?

Some women instinctively look through a gender lens when thinking about investing. For some women, it's a no-brainer on a theoretical level, but on a practical level they don't know where to start. And for other women, it is just not on the radar. Simply because you are a woman does not mean that gender-smart investing has to be a priority for you. If you are undecided or this is a concept that is new to you, as you think about your own position, there are some things you should know.

### It's a growing sector (and for good reasons)
Gender-smart investing is a growing sector that many sustainable or impact investors are interested in and one that is rapidly gaining traction across the world. In many developed markets, there are now a myriad of options popping up for the gender-smart investor, including angel

investment networks, retail-focused funds and venture capital vehicles – all with a gender focus.

How big are we talking? There have been some valiant efforts to put a stake in the ground so that we can measure the progress that has been made. For example, *Project Sage* – a collaboration between the Wharton Social Impact Initiative and Suzanne Biegel – researched and published a landscape analysis of structured private equity, venture capital and private debt vehicles with a gender lens in October 2017.[5] Subsequent research tracking and assessing year-on-year growth and trends in this space has followed.

In 2020, *Project Sage 3.0*, the latest iteration of the research, identified 138 total funds deploying capital with a gender lens, up 58.6 per cent from the 87 funds in 2019's *Project Sage 2.0*, and up 138 per cent from the 58 funds in the initial report.[6] Total capital raised has cleared $4.8 billion, more than doubling from *Project Sage 2.0*'s reported $2.2 billion. The true total is likely to be higher than this as some funds chose not to report funds raised.

Certainly, we see many of the large financial institutions get involved, with big banks, such as Bank of America, Merrill Lynch, UBS and Goldman Sachs, throwing their weight behind gender-lens investing. Asset managers such as Legal & General Investment Management and Columbia Threadneedle Investments have also started to engage, and many are launching tailored investment products (see below for some of these). Confirming this growing interest, Veris Wealth Partners conduct regular studies tracking vehicles such as mutual funds and ETFs that invest in listed companies that focus on gender. The most recent results indicate strong growth, as of 30 June 2019, investors had poured $3.4 billion into these vehicles, up from $2.4 billion in 2018.[7] That's quite a leap. As important, the size of the funds continued to grow, reflecting their growing popularity among individual and institutional investors. There were 10 investment products with over $100 million and six with over $250 million as of 30 June 2019.

## Women founders just don't get the cash

We know that the massive funding gap faced by women entrepreneurs is a global phenomenon. There are plenty of stats flying around and pretty much all of them are completely astounding.

For example, PitchBook found that while venture capital funding overall has surged in recent years, this hasn't been the case for female founders. By mid-2020, companies founded solely by women garnered only 2.1 per cent of total capital invested in venture-backed start-ups in the US.[8] What's worse, in Q3 2020, venture funding for female founders hit its lowest quarterly total in three years. It seems that in the face of uncertainty, many VCs have stayed closer to their networks, affecting women and minorities trying to break into their circle.[9]

Recent research by HSBC Private Banking found that more than a third of the world's women entrepreneurs have experienced gender bias when trying to raise capital for their business.[10] So, for many, gender-smart investing is about correcting this pathway and ensuring that women have access to the funding needed to grow their businesses.

## Gender diversity is good for economies

Supporters believe there is not only a pressing moral imperative to promote gender equality, but an economic one as well, with the potential to positively impact on global and regional economies. For example, according to strategy firm McKinsey, gender equality could add up to $28 trillion to the world's output by 2050, in a 'full potential' scenario in which women play identical roles in the labour markets to those of men.[11]

The trailblazing Christine Lagarde, former Managing Director of the IMF, in a 2019 article in the *Guardian*, highlighted research by the Fund which shows that women bring new skills to the workplace.[12] This helps to boost productivity as well as the size of the workforce. In countries ranked in the bottom 50 per cent for gender equality, the gains are thought to be substantial – an increase in the size of the economy by 35 per cent on average. Lagarde's point is clear:

> Things are changing. There was a time when women in the economy, women in employment, women in finance were not seen as macro-critical. That's no longer the case.

The evidence is stacking up as research continues to demonstrate the compelling case for gender diversity in the workforce, for overall economic growth, as well as improvements in innovation and productivity.

## Gender diversity is good for business

At the macroeconomic level, gender diversity is hugely beneficial – and so too at the company level. To date, much of the discussion on how this is implemented has focused on improving gender diversity at the board level and within senior management teams. In 2017, Larry Fink, BlackRock Chairman and CEO, wrote in his legendary annual open letter to CEOs that diverse boards 'are less likely to succumb to groupthink or miss new threats to a company's business model. And they are better able to identify opportunities that promote long-term growth'.[13]

The research we have on board and management diversity packs a punch whichever way you look at it. For example (and this is just a small selection of the research that is out there):

- MSCI found that US companies with at least three women on their boards had median increases of 37 per cent on earnings per share and 10 per cent in return on equity, over the five-year period of the study.[14] That is excellent financial performance.

- McKinsey has studied the relationship between diversity and corporate performance over a number of years and in its recent study noted that 'companies in the top quartile for gender diversity on their executive teams were 21 per cent more likely to experience above-average profitability than companies in the fourth quartile'.[15]

- In one of the most comprehensive pieces of research, S&P found that firms 'with female CEOs and CFOs have produced superior stock price performance, compared to the market average. In the 24 months post-appointment, female CEOs saw a 20 per cent increase in stock price momentum and female CFOs saw a 6 per cent increase in profitability and 8 per cent larger stock returns. These results are economically and statistically significant.'[16]

But it is not just about women in leadership positions. There are strong arguments for greater diversity at all levels of a company, from increasing productivity to higher levels of innovation, from reducing staff turnover to improving work–life balance.

## Women, leadership and corporate sustainability

I have often thought about the extent to which there may be a correlation between the number of women in leadership positions and the positive sustainability performance of a company. At this stage, it is mostly anecdotal and gut instinct, but I am convinced there is something in it.

For example, there was some fascinating research done by Chelsea Liu from the University of Adelaide, which found that companies with more gender-balanced boards are less often sued for breaching environmental laws. This gives further fuel to the argument that diversity is key to decision-making and that, in turn, this can influence the environmental performance of companies. Sure, it is only looking at the correlation between the gender makeup of corporate boards and their likelihood of having been sued on environmental grounds in subsequent years. However, it provides invaluable food for thought.[17]

Another exciting aspect is to consider the relationship between women in work and how this may positively shape product and service design as we move into a carbon-constrained and environmentally challenged world. This is directly relevant to gender-smart investing opportunities that are linked to products that capture the women's market (as per the second point on defining gender-smart investing above).

## What does this mean for sustainable investors?

The considerations I have outlined inevitably raise constructive questions about how to build more valuable and impactful business models, and how to leverage gender-smart investing to deliver on this. With our sustainable investor hats on, let's reiterate where this plays a role:

- Diversity and inclusion in the workplace matters, and this is not restricted simply to gender diversity. All kinds of diversity matter and bring benefits throughout companies and sectors.

- More women in leadership positions results in companies having stronger financial performance over time.

- Labour force participation by women increases when companies have balanced workplaces, including family-friendly policies, so having the right culture and work environment is essential.

- As investors, we play a critical role in promoting gender equality – using our voice to drive companies to understand the value and benefit of this is an exciting opportunity to bring about change.

When you look at gender-focused investment funds, we see many positive results. For example, Morningstar analysed the performance of 10 gender-focused funds in North America and Europe that invest in large cap companies (corporations with market capitalisation of $10 billion or greater). It found seven of these funds performed in the top quartiles of their categories.[18]

There are a number of phenomenal gender-lens investment managers setting up, many of which are performing very well. Take, for example, Nia Global Solutions launched in 2013 by Kristin Hull. Hull's focus is to bring activism and impact investment to the public markets. In doing so she developed Nia's six solutions-focused investment themes, weaving a gender lens throughout the investment thesis. Nia looks at companies that improve the lives of women and girls as defined by some of the SDGs and all holdings must have women in positions of leadership.

## KRISTIN HULL, PHD, FOUNDER AND CEO, NIA IMPACT CAPITAL

*Nia Impact Capital is a women-led impact investing firm, investing with an eye toward racial equity and a gender lens for an inclusive and sustainable economy.*

**Why did you decide to establish Nia Impact Capital?**

We are living in a time where we can't afford to not have our money aligned with our values and invested into the world in which we want to live. Nia means intention and purpose in Swahili, and our mission is to empower people to invest their money with purpose. I specifically wanted to provide a transparent and easy to understand investment vehicle where all of the companies are working on solutions to our largest risks, and that they all include diverse leadership.

**What have you learned about how women want to invest?**

Women want to invest into the world in which they want to live. Women understand that what we invest in grows, and so to have the capacity to invest in solutions-focused companies with purpose is important. Once we help connect the dots, women are quick to see that our investments are an extension of who we are, and so to have our values reflected in the companies in our portfolios is important. Women want to see themselves reflected in their portfolios as well, so to have companies with women in leadership is key.

**What advice do you have for a woman just starting her sustainable investment journey?**

Start where you feel most comfortable. This could be switching your bank to a local, more values-aligned institution, or it could be divesting from companies you find to be harmful.

Reach out for advice, and be sure to involve your friends. Mansplaining is real, and I see examples of this often, especially when women opt to move against the status quo, moving away from standard indexes and large banks, moving their money toward the solutions they care about. Be strong in your convictions and share your progress, as your story and example will be a powerful inspiration to others.

## OK, SO WHY AREN'T WE DOING MORE GENDER-SMART INVESTING?

There have been some amazing champions out there, pushing the analysis and evidence along, and societal discussions on women's empowerment have certainly helped push things forward too.

But we still have some work to do on perceptions. Research by Calvert Impact Capital found that lack of action in the impact investing market is partly due to the need to strengthen the business case for incorporating gender into investment decision-making.[19] Calvert also found that investors (men and women) are confused about how to incorporate gender into their process and analysis.

So, while there are volumes of data out there that show that companies investing more in women do better financially and economically, we need to shout about it and make sure we get heard. We also need to work at getting more sophisticated data that fully explores the nuances of gender diversity on performance, and not just financial performance at that. We are seeing some bold fund managers move forward in offering gender-smart investment products and this is only set to grow over time.

Gender washing is a concern, with the likelihood that companies will regard diversity as a box-ticking exercise. How do we avoid this? As with all types of 'washing' in the sustainable investment world, we need to keep working on the rigorous measurement of outcomes of these investments.[20]

---

### SUZANNE BIEGEL, FOUNDER OF CATALYST AT LARGE AND CO-FOUNDER OF THE GENDERSMART INVESTING SUMMIT

*Catalyst at Large provides consultancy, speaking and facilitation in the arena of gender lens investing. This spans the intersection of investment, philanthropy, international development and entrepreneurship.*

*The GenderSmart Investing Summit brings together investors and investment influencers with diverse perspectives – across geographies, asset classes and sectors. What all Summit participants have in common is their ability to influence the movement of significant capital with a gender lens.*

**Why are investors not doing more on gender-smart investing?**

There are many reasons why the market is not doing more on gender-smart investing. There are unseen and undervalued opportunities as well as unseen and undervalued risks. We have a lot of eyes to open. Bias – conscious and unconscious. Power – those who have it are not often quick to share it. Structural barriers – Investment

Policy Statements that need to be updated, investment processes and tools that need an upgrade. Investment teams that need diversification and coaching, as well as incentive systems to revisit. Many of the most exciting new funds are also from first-time fund managers, and there are historical structural reasons for lack of access to capital for first-time managers. Thus, change is hard. The advisory community – wealth managers, financial advisors, investment consultants – need these products on their platforms and need to know how to advise on them or sell them. Investors, not yet knowledgeable, don't know what to ask for or how to ask for it. Those are just a few!

**What can female investors do to get involved in gender-smart investing?**

Female investors – and I teach a lot of them – can learn about what they already own. See how those investments match up with their values. They can learn about the products that are available today that meet their financial risk, return and liquidity goals and their investment capacity and vision. They can talk with their advisors about what they can get, and move their money if they can't get it from their platforms. They can demand that their pension fund choices include a sophisticated gender lens; they can back new fund managers and play a catalytic role into new funds.

If they have a donor-advised fund, or they want to start one, they can use philanthropic capital in some places to do gender-smart investing. They can get training in areas they're interested in, and join networks and syndicates in their geographic regions (there are so many, from Dubai to Lagos to Jakarta to Chattanooga at this point).

## GENDER-SMART INVESTING IN ACTION

Tracy Gray, Managing Partner at The 22 Fund (formerly The 22 Capital Group), Founder at We Are Enough, Executive in Residence at LACI, puts it so well:

> Whether you have $25 or $25 million, whether you have a piggy-bank, or you own a bank, you can invest with your values by investing with a gender-lens.

Despite the challenges, there are many wonderful and inspiring examples of how we can invest in gender-smart ways. If you want to invest in companies based on how well they integrate women, there are funds that follow such strategies. These examples sit across asset classes, including private and public, investment strategies, regions and markets. Here are just a few examples, but there are so many more out there, so don't think of this as a definitive list, just an illustration of how wide the movement is going.

### Women of the World Endowment (WoWE)

WoWE is a disruptive innovator in the gender investment landscape seeking to demonstrate that allocating assets with a gender-lens investing (GLI) screen yields at least the same risk-adjusted returns as other investment strategies, while delivering impact for women and girls and the communities they empower. WoWE does so through complementary impact and financial engineering capabilities, focusing on ensuring investors have access to the insights, data and best practices necessary to develop a meaningful GLI strategy. The model drives continual learning and improvement through five centres of excellence, each of which focuses on addressing issues core to women and girls.

The unique objective of WoWE is that funding comes from multiple sources – from high-net-worth individuals to institutional funders, from foundations through to retail investors. The capital raised is game-changing because WoWE is seeking to drive a paradigm shift that ensures women are front and centre of our financial markets, fundamentally changing the way we think about investment strategies.

### PATIENCE MARIME-BALL, FOUNDER, WOWE

*Women of the World Endowment (WoWE) invests at the intersection of gender and some of today's most pressing social and environmental issues. WoWE is singularly focused on driving impact at scale to improve the lives of women and girls in the context of an institutional-quality structure that can deliver market-rate risk-adjusted returns.*

**Tell us about WoWE and what inspired you.**

After conversations with friends, sponsors and mentors, I landed on the idea of a Women's Endowment – the scale of which could really change the way we think about gender-lens investing. WoWE involves, actually it requires, a large pool of capital that has the flexibility to invest in gender-lens assets across the capital spectrum, but, at the same time, influence other institutional pools of capital to catalyse positive change towards women and girls.

**What is at the heart of WoWE?**

Over a number of years, I have become acutely aware of the fact that entities focused on women's empowerment, whether NGOs or profit-maximising vehicles, all face a common problem – lack of access to capital. This issue above all informs the lack of scalability – too much time is spent raising money or operating with tight budgets, so achieving scale and thereby impact is a mighty mountain to climb. Today, we are in a moment where we can build for systemic change.

**In 10 years' time, what do you want to have achieved with WoWE? What is the impact you are looking for?**

I truly believe that Women of the World Endowment will disrupt the gender landscape by developing, supporting and catalysing tipping points in favour of investment in women and girls. A successful raise of the Endowment signals potential for gender parity and for social impact through investment. The power of this cannot be underestimated.

We are also building a knowledge-driven approach – a robust hub-and-spoke ecosystem of intellectual capital and best practice implementation – because this will accelerate the delivery cycle of benefits and impact. Success is about driving confidence across the women's market, adding value to those investments through shared know-how and tools, the application of technology and data-driven decision-making.

## Japan Impact Investment II Limited Partnership

Japan Impact Investment II LP pulls together the expertise and resources of Shinsei Impact, Mizuho Bank and Japan's

Social Impact Investment Foundation to launch a fund that invests in early- to later-stage companies focused on childcare, nursing care and flexible working-based businesses. In its first closing, the fund raised ¥2.2 billion (more than $20 million), with the objective of improving knowledge and understanding of impact investing in Japan, positioning it as an 'economic country solving social challenges' while securing both economic and social returns.[21]

## We Are Jane

We Are Jane is a Benelux-focused venture fund, billing itself as 'an investment fund by women, for women'. What's really great about We Are Jane is that it's led by an all-woman management team and gets half of its investment capital from female investors. The idea behind the fund is to provide growth capital to businesses with a female owner or CEO, seeking companies with a proven track record of success.[22]

## Pax Ellevate Global Women's Leadership Fund

Pax Ellevate's Invest in Women strapline says it all: 'If you believe women should be better represented in the business world, you can put your money to work.'

The Global Women's Leadership Fund is one of the first mutual funds that invests in 'the highest-rated companies in the world for advancing women through gender diversity on their boards and in executive management'. The premise behind the fund is that it allows investors to focus on closing the gender gap by explicitly looking for companies that value women's leadership, aiming to be 'part of the solution, rather than part of the problem'.[23]

## RobecoSAM Global Gender Equality Impact Equities

Another example is the RobecoSAM Global Gender Equality Impact Equities, which is based on the belief that investing in gender equality creates a positive societal impact. The investment strategy looks for companies that are recognising and acting on the strategic importance of improving gender equality and in the belief that this will improve their competitive advantage and deliver long-term shareholder returns. RobecoSAM also acknowledges the link with the achievement of certain of the UN Sustainable Development Goals through investing in companies that 'exhibit strength in the retention of female talent, equal remuneration and employee well-being'.

## Legal & General Investment Management's GIRL fund

The L&G Future World Gender in Leadership UK Index Fund – known widely as the 'GIRL fund' – is a tracker fund backing British firms that have a greater gender balance. The fund looks for companies with better gender diversity scores, backing 350 of the UK's largest companies, and aims to make an impact while also delivering income and growth. The good news is that, since its launch in May 2018, it has beaten the market.[24]

# BUILDING A GENDER-SMART INVESTMENT STRATEGY

So, if gender-smart investing sounds like your gig, what will you do now?

There is no one right answer, no straight path to incorporating gender into your investments. To that extent, you get to define your own objectives. Don't let that ambiguity put you off because it's not rocket science and it is certainly not niche (women, niche? Come on!). In fact, quite the opposite. As with most aspects of sustainable investing, it makes good business sense and it's just good investing.

One challenge to be aware of – and perhaps you have already picked up on it when reading about the available investment funds – many of the discussions are still focusing on women in leadership positions, either at the board or senior management level. We still have some way to go in terms of other dimensions to gender-smart investing.

## Back to the Sustainable Development Goals – SDG 5 to be specific!

Gender sits as a theme throughout the Sustainable Development Goals because achieving most of them will have a direct and positive effect on the lives of women and girls around the world. And of course, SDG 5 – Gender Equality ('achieve gender equality and empower all women and girls') – is fully committed to women, so go for it.

My suggestion is that you look at SDG 5, the targets and the KPIs and identify what matters to you. Take this thinking and ask yourself:

- What am I looking for in terms of impact on the lives of women and girls?

- To what extent is leadership and governance diversity important to me?

- Am I looking for direct impact on women and their families?

- What gender-specific issues do I want to address, such as access to education and/or health services?

- Do I want to support female entrepreneurship, and female founders specifically?

- When I look at a company, is gender incorporated into its mission, strategy and operations? Is there management and reporting of progress against stated gender goals?

- To what extent does the company design products and services with women in mind?

## Be an angel

In Chapter 3 we introduced the concept of angel investing and in Chapter 5 we talked about the relevance of angels to the sustainable investing world.

If you are remotely excited about gender-smart investing, I would suggest checking out what is going on in the angel investing world on the gender front. We are seeing the emergence of women angel investor groups across the world explicitly seeking out female founders and entrepreneurs to support. This is driven by a keen interest in addressing the massive funding gap that female founders face.

Angel investing with a gender lens is something I got into a few years ago, and I have never looked back. As I mentioned before, angel investing is high risk but there are many gains. One of the most significant gains for me has been on a personal level – I have connected with smart, passionate and amazing women from all over the world. These women have all been driven by the desire to make change happen – and to put their money where their mouth is when it comes to supporting the sisterhood. One thing I have learned when I sit in a room with female angel investors is that we do our homework, we work hard to understand the companies and the women we invest in. We think through societal problems and subsequently seek out solutions to these problems. We think and we work together as a team.

If this sounds appealing to you, check out if you have any local women angel investor networks or funds – most do not require high entry tickets so it might be an accessible way to connect with like-minded women and make an impact at the same time. This can also mean you are actually able to invest affordably in some amazing concepts that are otherwise overlooked.

### HEATHER HENYON, FOUNDER, WAIN (WOMEN'S ANGEL INVESTOR NETWORK, DUBAI, UAE), AND FOUNDING GENERAL PARTNER, MINDSHIFT CAPITAL

*Mindshift Capital is a global, women-run venture firm investing in amazing women-led companies solving big problems with sophisticated solutions. Mindshift partners take an active, collaborative role in the growth of portfolio companies with focus on successful exit pathways.*

#### Why did you set up WAIN and then move on to Mindshift Capital?

I started WAIN because there were very few women angel investors in the MENA (Middle East/North Africa) region and I saw an opportunity given that half of the new business founders are women. I also wanted women to feel more self-confident about their financial literacy, which was an outcome of being part of the investment process in a start-up. As I learned more about venture capital, I realised that there was a gap for female founders at the venture capital round for similar reasons as the seed round gap (2 per cent of the VC funding in 2018 in the US went to women-led start-ups) – again, very few women VC partners (8 per cent of VC partners in the US are women). I created Mindshift to solve this.

#### What are the main challenges that female founders face? Are there regional differences?

I see it across my 100 investments in the US, Europe and the Middle East – it takes female founders twice as long to raise half the amount of capital as the guys, and at a lower valuation. We target the post-seed gap at Mindshift – many female founders don't raise enough capital at seed to hit the milestones needed to raise a Series A round and therefore end up raising a bridge round between the seed and A rounds.

> **What can we, as female investors, do to move the needle on investing in women entrepreneurs?**
>
> 'Funding is the new feminism.' We need more women investors at all stages – seed, VC, PE – especially as women are the fastest-growing segment of entrepreneurs globally.

## YOU ARE AT THE START OF AN EXCITING JOURNEY – JOIN US

The issue of gender diversity and closing the equality gap is not going away – nor should it, until we have the balance that we are all striving for. This means that gender-smart investment products and initiatives will continue to grow. Some governments and some institutional investors are looking to expedite the process and we can play a role as retail investors. There are so many useful resources out there if you want to learn more, and amazing women in the gender space to follow. Take the first step and join the growing sisterhood – now is your chance to get ahead of the game and make the change we want to see.

## ELEVEN

# WHO YOU GONNA CALL? – THE
# ROLE OF THE FINANCIAL ADVISOR

On numerous occasions throughout this book, I have referred to the importance of speaking with a financial advisor or investment professional as you craft your way forward. There are good reasons for this. A financial advisor can assist you in making sense of the investment world and examining your unique financial situation from a trained and experienced perspective. A good advisor can provide personalised financial information so that you make decisions that are aligned with your broader financial goals. This may include investing, saving for retirement, estate planning and other solutions such as life insurance and long-term care insurance.

## WOMEN AND FINANCIAL ADVISORS

However, many women struggle to engage with a financial advisor – and this may occur for a variety of reasons.

There is growing research that indicates that women may not trust a financial advisor, with plenty of anecdotal evidence of women feeling condescended to. For example, a recent survey of women in the UK found that a third said that they have been 'patronised' when dealing with the industry.[1] Another piece of research found that a whopping 73 per cent of women felt their financial advisor misunderstood them.[2]

Whether or not a financial advisor is male or female also seems to be a potential sticking point, with some evidence that some women prefer to work with female advisors. This is an important finding to unpack, given that the majority of financial advisors are men – for example, in the US, male financial advisors comprise approximately three-quarters of the industry.[3]

One thing is clear – the financial and investment needs of women clearly differ from those of men. As we explored in earlier chapters, women typically earn less than men over the lifetime of their career, they tend to live longer and take more unpaid leave than men. These factors and other circumstances contribute to very different profiles and needs that perhaps many financial advisors do not take fully into account. Perhaps women also look for a different type of interaction than men, with some research suggesting women prefer face-to-face advice, even though financial advisors may not be delivering according to their expectations.

This tricky relationship gets even stickier when you bring in the topic of sustainable investing (and be aware, this is a challenge for both women and men). It seems that many financial advisors are somewhat of a roadblock on the sustainable investment front. Increasingly, many now understand the importance of the topic but still struggle with bridging the gap between idea and implementation.

The purpose of this chapter is to support you in understanding what to look for from your relationship with a financial advisor, generally and from a sustainable investing perspective. It is very simply structured to cover, first, the role of a financial advisor, and second, what this can mean for you as you commence your sustainable investment journey.

## WHAT IS THE ROLE OF A FINANCIAL ADVISOR?

I don't know about you, but I didn't really know what a financial advisor was until I was in my early 30s. And honestly that is only because he introduced himself to me and asked me to an exclusive dinner event for clients! I suppose I was momentarily flattered that I might be considered worthy of buttering up for business opportunities. To this day, I have no idea how he got my name or number.

It is essential to start with a good understanding of what a financial advisor is and how they can provide you with the support you need. A financial advisor isn't the end game in itself but can be used effectively to facilitate more informed financial decision-making. Of course, you can also go to your bank for some of this, but it really does depend on the services your particular bank provides and the level of cash you will need for it to engage with you as a client.

## What can a financial advisor help with?

A financial advisor can help with a range of things, obviously depending on your financial circumstances and where you are in your life. This may include:

- Assisting you in prioritising your financial goals and creating a personalised financial strategy, including customised solutions to help you pursue these goals.

- Regularly reviewing and rebalancing your portfolio as both you and the markets change over time, helping keep you on track with your goals.

- Supporting you in making rational decisions based on your circumstances and taking some of the emotions out of money decisions.

- Working with you to help figure out saving for your retirement and when to withdraw your assets according to your needs.

- Depending on where you live, help in considering potential tax consequences of your investment strategy and withdrawals.

## Technology and financial advisors

In Chapter 12, we explore in greater depth the influence

that technology is having on the financial industry and also the role that financial advisors play. Technology is undeniably changing most aspects of the investment process and as this automation happens, the soft skills of financial advisors become increasingly more prominent. These skills include attributes such as the ability to listen, level of empathy, relationship-building strengths, communications and creativity.

Sustainable investing is an area where a financial advisor can prove their value to clients. In this field, experience and judgement become more critical because the decision made will require expertise and have more impact (and potentially carry higher risk). If you can find a trusted advisor to help you deal with challenges such as investment uncertainty, limited data and implied risk – all of which are relevant to sustainable investment approaches – it could really play in your favour as you develop into a sustainable investor.

Technology does not do away with the need for human interaction and advice. As the industry evolves, perhaps the most important skills of the future will be those that are solutions-based, being able to understand a client's needs and then to enable the delivery of investor-driven outcomes.[4]

## What is a virtual financial advisor?

A virtual financial advisor is pretty much what you expect it to be – a qualified advisor, but one who leverages digital technology to provide tailored services to clients.

The virtual model replaces networks of branch offices with a central hub through which clients can be served via telephone, video conference and digital tools.[5] For the investment industry, this has enabled wealth managers to access clients who have historically been challenging to serve in a cost-effective manner, particularly that middle wealth bracket. In the next chapter we also explore the role of fintech and how this is transforming the sustainable investment landscape, particularly when it comes to advisors.

## What's important to you in a financial advisor?

So, we know that women face a few challenges when engaging with advisors. How can we improve this? With so few women in the financial industry, and as financial advisors themselves, the industry itself has some work to do on hiring in more women, and at all levels. This will build a more diverse work culture and help shift from a male-centric mode of thinking.

If you are considering working with an investment professional, there are a few thoughts you may want to keep in mind as you travel down the road of finding the right one:

### How important is it to have emotional engagement?

As the industry evolves, and as technology has an increasing impact, emotional engagement may become more relevant to you. When you choose a financial advisor to work with, make sure you have this personal connection and you feel comfortable in how you relate. At the same time, consider the role that you want technology to play in your own investment decision-making. It doesn't have to be an all-or-nothing situation.

*Be aware of potential biases that a financial advisor may have*[6]

For example, these may include:

- Personal bias – this may be reflected in the way that an advisor personally engages with women. Some women have reported that they feel overlooked because an advisor wants to speak to the 'man of the house' and dismisses their role in financial decision-making.

- Familiarity bias – the advisor may only deal with certain types of investment products (e.g. equity investments) and may not actually be comfortable talking about other types. This also has relevance to our sustainable investment discussion which we will cover in more detail below.

- Short-term bias – an advisor may be overly focused on the short term, not thinking adequately through what may be desirable in the long term. This may not fit with your own needs – they should be reflecting your financial goals and your investment strategy. Sustainable investing is about thinking about long-term impacts and trends, so this is worth bearing in mind.

- Commission bias – this relates to an advisor earning commission on certain investment products rather than charging for advisory services. This can obviously influence the advisor's recommendations and is something you should be aware of. Over the last couple of decades, there have been some serious breaches when it comes to commission-based advice and regulators in some countries have made efforts to clean this up. Most investors now opt for paid-for advisory services to avoid the commission issue.

## Do you want to work with a female advisor?

With so few female financial advisors, it is no wonder that many clients want this situation to change. Also, given some of the issues that women face with male advisors, you can understand why many women may gravitate towards female advisors.

Of course, a financial advisor must be properly trained and experienced. However, at the same time, you want to work with someone who can empathise with your situation, understand your money hang-ups and whom you can trust with your dreams and fears. Let's not forget that money and your investment intentions touch on very intimate aspects of your life. It makes sense that you may want to work with someone you feel most comfortable with, in the same way that many women may prefer a female doctor or therapist.

The good news is that more women are moving into financial advisory roles so it should become increasingly easy to find a female advisor who fits what you are looking for.[7] There are also a number of female-focused advisory firms emerging and wealth management companies led by women to deliver services specifically for women.

*What is the difference between a financial advisor and a financial planner?*

If you have decided to seek professional help with your finances, you should be aware of the difference between a financial advisor and a financial planner, although the lines are becoming increasingly blurred. The important distinction to keep in mind is that a financial planner is a type of financial advisor, but a financial advisor is not necessarily a financial planner.

A financial planner tends to take a more holistic approach with clients. The work is likely to be more in-depth and comprehensive in the sense that it may involve thinking through long-term financial goals – from graduation through to retirement – and managing investment portfolios accordingly. An advisor is anyone who advises someone on certain financial matters and can be quite broadly applied to include a broker or an insurance agent, as well as an investment advisor.

You may also hear about someone called a 'financial coach'. This is a newer concept and certainly more encompassing of life goals and how your financial plan should fit around these. As with other types of coaching (life, career, etc.), a financial coach aims to empower clients to take responsibility for their decisions and sometimes also work out how to hold yourself accountable.

While we are on the topic, many banks offer customers the use of their financial advisors for investments. This may mean lower fee transactions or other incentives offered by the bank, as well as the benefits that come from having an existing relationship. There are likely to be some minimum amounts that the bank will want you to hold with it before offering investment services, but it is an option worth exploring.

At the end of the day, you have to find the solution that is right for you. Also, make sure you understand how the advisor makes money and the fees that are charged, based on trades, meetings and services. You may even want to consider interviewing the advisor first to ensure you are a good match.

## SUSTAINABLE INVESTING AND FINANCIAL ADVISORS

Historically, financial advisors have not been good promoters of sustainable investing with their clients. Why is this? There are a number of reasons, but probably the biggest is a lack of knowledge or understanding of what sustainable investing is, or the opportunities it can provide to the individual investor. Even against a background of notable growing consumer enthusiasm, that certainly hasn't been matched by advisor attitudes. This is changing.

### Why are advisors not bringing up sustainable investing with their clients?

Allianz Global Investors published the results of an interesting survey in which it found only 14 per cent of investors surveyed had even discussed ESG as an investment strategy with their advisors, and a whopping 61 per cent of them had to bring up the subject themselves.[8]

This was also confirmed in a recent study by the Rockefeller Foundation which found that investors do not feel that their advisors are delivering trusted impact investment advice (note – this study was focused on impact investing). Four out of 10 investors cite 'difficulty sourcing credible investment advice' as their biggest challenge to increasing their allocation to impact investing.[9]

A lot of this is happening because advisors simply don't have the knowledge or understanding. It may be that they are intimidated by the language used in the sustainable investing world, perhaps finding it divisive or politicised.[10] They may not have the expertise to communicate clearly with clients about sustainable investing concepts and actions. It may also be the case that some advisors are cautious not to 'push' their views on their clients. But of course, the limited availability of sustainable and impact investment products will also be a barrier preventing advisors from being more proactive.

## The changing landscape

Despite these barriers, investors want sustainable investing options, so the message is clear – financial advisors need to catch up. Thankfully, we are now seeing more and more advisors get on board and begin to incorporate sustainability and ESG considerations into their processes. Interestingly, there is much less nervousness among retail investors about the performance of sustainable investments than there used to be, and this is opening up conversations that are moving the sector along.

When a financial advisor gets it right, it can really enhance the quality of the relationship with the client. It is a massive opportunity for an advisor to stand out and differentiate themselves. However, to get to that point, an advisor must be both well versed and fully comfortable with sustainable investment concepts, measurements and products to enable them to really understand what their client is looking for and offer the level of support she is looking for.

It is also worth bearing in mind that, while there is currently no regulatory requirement for financial advisors to raise sustainable investment and ESG issues with their clients, this is likely to change. And soon. Nobody wants retail investors to be left behind in a world that is rapidly waking up to massive investment risks like climate change.

## Choosing an advisor to support you on your sustainable investment journey

When it comes to choosing a financial advisor to work with as you carve out your sustainable investment journey, it is worth spending a bit of time doing your research and thinking about who might be the best fit for you. The very first question to ask is – what do they understand as sustainable investing? This sounds obvious, but it's an important question to ask because if this is not aligned with your definition, perhaps you want to look elsewhere. You don't want to spend your time battling over definitions and terms.

Expect an advisor to begin with what you are really passionate about and to have that conversation directly with you. It is an important starting point because you are driven by your personal values and you want your advisor to recognise this. Here are a few additional pointers and tips to make the process of finding a suitable advisor more straightforward:

*Fully understand their experience*
When you choose a financial advisor, make sure that you correctly understand their experience in terms of their knowledge, but also how they get compensated. Compensation matters because it indicates the extent to which they are incentivised to recommend or direct you towards certain funds.

Part of understanding their experience is also learning about their approach and then reflecting on how this will fit with the kind of relationship you are looking for. For example, do you want to be intimately involved in the investment decisions or do you prefer an advisor to take the lead? To what extent will the advisor work with you to come up with customised approaches that take into account your personal values? Are they willing to support you in exploring new sustainable and impact investment opportunities?

You may also want to understand what other kind of clients they work for, and whether this includes providing sustainable investment advice. Do they have a strong track record in supporting clients with sustainable investing? This is all part of your personal due diligence.

*Look for advisors who have made an effort to learn
about sustainable investing*

We are seeing efforts to improve and educate financial advisors on sustainable investing. Given this, it is worth asking any potential advisor if they have done (or heard of) any of these formal courses.

For example, the Money Management Institute and Morningstar now run a sustainable investing curriculum which 'provides financial advisors with an introduction to the fundamentals, principles and practices of sustainable and environmental, social and governance (ESG) investing.' If your advisor is a CFA (Chartered Financial Analyst), the CFA Institute now runs a series of courses on 'ESG Investing and SRI Education' so perhaps ask whether she has taken these.

*Get to know your advisor*

Outside of a potential advisor's experience and education, you may also want to get to know them better in terms of both your personality fit and values, as well as their knowledge on specific issues that are of concern to you – for example, climate change, gender diversity, social justice and so on. If environmental issues are a top priority for you, make sure you are connecting with someone who understands what these are in the broader context. Even better if they are concerned about these too. Greenwashing, impact washing, etc. are also relevant to this situation and we need to be aware that, while many people are jumping on the bandwagon, we cannot undervalue what a true expert and advisor brings to us.

## Ask about metrics

Transparency is important and having the metrics in place to help understand the impact of our investments is a critical component of what we are doing. Don't underestimate the importance of finding a financial advisor who understands what kind of metrics you may be looking for, but also knows how to communicate these with you. You will want to see that they understand your personal objectives and therefore what this means you are looking for in terms of measurements and metrics. This will also reflect how a financial advisor measures success in the broader context, so it is a question worth asking.

---

### BONNY LANDERS, SENIOR CLIENT ADVISOR, WEALTH IMPACT STRATEGY, BRIDGES FUND MANAGEMENT

*Bridges Fund Management Ltd. is a fund manager that specialises in sustainable and impact investing. It invests in business, properties and social sector organisations, with a focus on four impact themes: health and wellbeing, education and skills, sustainable living and under-served markets*

**How do you think that financial advisors can support female investors to take action on sustainable investing?**

The most important rule for the financial advisor (FA) is to Know Your Client. This rule also leads to the best role the financial advisor can have – that of the Trusted Advisor. FAs need to understand that, when a client asks about sustainable, responsible or impact investing, it is coming from the heart – studies and surveys show that women are

---

especially interested in ensuring that their investments are benefiting society. Financial advisors need to respond to the client's goals in order to retain them as clients as well.

Moreover, there is now enough empirical evidence and academic research to support taking into account sustainability factors when making investment decisions that financial advisors will be in breach of their fiduciary duties if they ignore them. FAs can respond positively to anyone requesting sustainable investments by first ensuring that they understand how the client defines 'sustainable investments' and then to compare the ever-increasing range of products which match the client's definition. Financial advisors must still use the traditional risk/return criteria in portfolio construction but should now add an impact analysis – what are the positive and negative impacts of the underlying investments, especially those which have a direct effect on the financial performance of the investments as well as the indirect impacts which may respond to the goals or concerns of the client.

**What would be your advice to a woman meeting with her bank or financial advisor for the first time to talk about sustainable investing?**

Any client should reflect on the following questions before meeting with a financial advisor:

1. What are my core values? – i.e. what do I most care about and what can I not abide? – these answers will help your FA to see how to align your investments with your values (e.g. if you want to see greater equality in the world, you may wish to emphasise investments which contribute to creating livelihoods, access to education and financial inclusion and avoid industries which may exacerbate poverty such as gambling and alcohol).

2. What are my financial needs? – i.e. how much income do I need at present or how much growth do I need over the longer term for my retirement? – this profile

will help your FA to understand your financial goals and to understand your risk appetite over time.

3. How do I define what success will look like, both in financial as well as impact terms? – these definitions are critical for the FA to know how you will measure performance.

**What market myths need to be busted on sustainable investing? How can we be prepared?**

I think our job is getting easier and easier – academics are helping to put to bed the myth that one gives up financial return to invest sustainably.[11] The Global Reporting Initiative and the Sustainability Accounting Standards Board are helping us to obtain the necessary information to analyse company sustainability data and to allow us to compare companies within peer groups. The UN-supported PRI is signing up the majority of asset managers to the Responsible Investment pledge.

We investors have much more support now to ensure we have the products and the processes to enable all of us to incorporate sustainability criteria into our investment decision-making, and to verify the outcomes. This also helps us to decide which financial advisor to choose – if an FA does not encourage you to discuss your values, your goals and your needs, let alone your wish to increase your sustainable, responsible or impact investments, find another advisor – there are now lots who have both the training and the understanding to help you!

## JULIA DREBLOW, FOUNDER, SRI SERVICES AND FUND ECOMARKET

*SRI Services is a UK-based independent company devoted to advancing retail Sustainable and Responsible Investment (SRI) funds. Its purpose is to encourage – and help facilitate – the expansion of this area in order to help effect positive environmental and social change and meet individual investors' personal values-based needs better. SRI Services is not authorised to offer investment advice and does not deal directly with individual investors. SRI Services offers its free-to-use fund tool Fund EcoMarket – set up to help financial advisers and other intermediaries to understand and compare sustainable, responsible and ethical investment fund options.*

**When it comes to sustainable investing, what are the biggest hurdles that women face?**

The culture in investment is to see things as all about numbers. I think this is probably off-putting for many women – and of course it represents a major market failure because it is simply untrue. Investors own companies. Companies have major environmental and social impacts. It stands to reason therefore that investors should consider the 'often hard to measure' environmental and social implications of where they invest – but many do not.

Until very recently, the culture of the investment industry has belittled those who think otherwise. My impression is that, although there are many men who find this abhorrent, women who want to look beyond the numbers are more numerous and so find the culture in investment pretty off-putting. Add to that the fact that exam boards have overlooked this area for years (despite regular attempts to encourage them to focus on it) and regulators have been pretty much blind to the interconnectivity of investment and the 'real world'. This has changed since the world signed up to the Paris Agreement – but there is still a very long way to go.

**Why are financial advisors not doing more to support women interested in sustainable investing? What is holding them back?**

It is not just women who financial advisors are failing in sustainable investing. Many advisors fail everyone in this area – if they care about environmental and social issues. This is not, however, necessarily the advisors' fault as their focus is largely shaped by a combination of training and regulation. So, as these areas largely overlook the context within which investment exists, the more 'humane' sides of investment struggle to be heard.

With regard to women more specifically, I am not sure the culture generally is a good fit. It could be (and it should be) that the investment world is diverse, flexible and innovative – COVID may turn out to be helpful in this regard but it remains to be proven. But it isn't. The prevailing 'make money at any cost' culture does not appeal to most women – so even for women who know little about investment and probably even less about sustainable investment, they will nonetheless spot that the way the system operates is 'off centre'.

A further factor has been the way people have commented about sustainable and ethical investment over the decades – implying it is a form of charity and that the funds will fail. In reality it is hard to think of anything that is further from the truth. Funds that focus on ESG-type issues do more investment research than other funds, not less – so very often their results are better, not worse. It is wrong to generalise of course, as there will be times when, for example, a fund that avoids coal, oil and gas may struggle to compete with a fund that invests in these areas if those sectors are 'flavour of the month' – but to my mind that does not make them either acceptable to support or a good long-term bet. We know things must change, so such incidents will hopefully be very short-lived.

**What are your top tips for women discussing sustainable investing with their advisor or bank?**

Firstly – do not expect advisors to encourage you down this route. Although the area is increasingly popular, many financial advisors still know little about the area and so feel uncomfortable talking about it. (This is not unsolvable of course an hour or two on my website looking at fund options and following links would sort that out.)

The next is not to be fooled by myths that have emerged, fostered by those with an interest in preserving the status quo. For example, it has always made me smile when people pick on a particular fund as an example of why the area does not make sense to support – forgetting that in all sectors there are funds that do better than others dependent on market conditions and other numerous factors. The SRI sector is no different than any other in that regard.

Another area to be wary of is greenwash. This worrying trend has grown substantially recently and all of a sudden pretty much everyone is claiming to be an expert. It is true that there have been some superb fund launches recently that really add to consumer choice – but others are sadly overhyped greenwash. My recommendation would be to 'look under the bonnet' to read what the fund manager says they actually do (there is no single correct strategy – diversity is not the problem, as it is welcome!). If you can't find any information about fund strategies – where a fund invests and why – or their voting strategies then move on.

And finally, if you are interested in this area you need to say so. It may soon be obligatory for advisors to discuss this area with clients, but until that happens do not expect it. Be extra careful of advisors who can only offer a single ethical or sustainable option. The chances of that single strategy being precisely what you are looking for are tiny. If you do not have an advisor, you can look at the 'direct' platforms, such as Interactive Investor, which are increasingly trying to help clients understand this area.

# TWELVE

## TECHNOLOGY – A GAME-CHANGER FOR SUSTAINABLE INVESTORS?

Historically, wealth management and investing have only really been accessible for those with substantial assets, those with lots of cash in the bank and those in a position to command the attention of private bankers and wealth managers. However, technological advances permit us the opportunity to potentially rewrite the definition of who can be included in the investing world.

Here's the thing. Technology not only has the potential to democratise WHO can invest. It also has the potential to allow us to decide HOW and WHERE to invest. Whatever way you look at this, it has massive implications for the world of sustainable investing and investors like you and me.

The purpose of this chapter is to give you a sense of how technology is impacting on the financial industry and to introduce how this is manifesting itself in sustainable investing. I then shine a spotlight on some of the tools and platforms currently out there, in the hope that you may start to look at these and potentially find ways to leverage them in your own sustainable investment journey.

## LET'S START AT THE BEGINNING – WHAT IS FINTECH?

'Fintech', a term you might well have heard mentioned, is new technology and innovation that aims to compete with traditional financial methods in the delivery of financial services. Fintech has been transforming the financial industry for a number of years now, throwing a curveball at traditional (and age-old) business and service delivery models. The result has been some major shifts in ways of thinking and doing things.

### How does technology affect us as investors?
For you and me, developments in fintech are central for four key reasons (there are probably more but let's stick with these for now).

### Opening up and democratising investing
Because technology is accessible by the majority of people, this is opening up opportunities that have not been available to many of us before. In the context of investment, the result is that we can democratise access to investment products, platforms and services. Investing is no longer just for the wealthy. Investing is becoming accessible for those with small amounts of money to put aside.

*Facilitating access to sustainable investing in particular*
The range of automated investment services, including robo-advisors and providers of low-cost exchange-traded funds, is making sustainable investing increasingly accessible to everyday investors. Tech is supporting financial experts in demystifying sustainable investing, as well as making it easier and more affordable for female investors to build and manage their sustainable investment portfolios.

*Improving transparency and access to information*
Technology is supporting the level of transparency across both the financial and the corporate world. This is allowing investors to make more informed decisions. For sustainable investors, real-time information on sustainability performance is providing us with data and indicators that allow us to make proactive decisions on where to move our capital in alignment with our values. Given we know that female investors are keen sustainable investors, this can only benefit us.

*Using tech to connect with women*
I have already touched on the challenges that some women face when engaging with the financial industry, and in Chapter 11 we talked about women's relationship with financial advisors, which has not always been positive. Technological advances offer us a pathway to circumvent this, to connect and communicate with women in different ways from the past. This is all about changing the nature

of communication, relationships and customisation of services that fit best for women today.[1]

## LET'S GET INTO THE WEEDS

Before looking at who is doing what out there, let us take a moment to run through some of the key developments, issues and themes on the fintech front – and, most importantly, how this currently shapes or has the potential to shape our thinking on sustainable investing.

### Robo-advisors

Robo-advisors harness the power of big data through automating financial advice and wealth management with minimal human intervention. Robo-advisors are a type of financial advisor, in effect, providing investment management services online. It's all about minimising the amount the client (the investor) needs to interact with a human being. How do they do this? Well, advice is based on algorithms. Underlying this is a complex software program that leverages the algorithms to automatically allocate, manage and optimise the investors' assets. This definition works very well – a robo-advisor is:

> a self-guided online wealth management service that provides automated investment advice at low costs and low account minimums, employing portfolio management algorithms.[2]

Since making a public appearance back in 2008, robo-advisors have rapidly increased in popularity, making it much easier for individuals to manage their assets personally. This is where the democratisation theme comes in. There are now robo-advisory companies all over the world and assets under management are expected to grow massively over the coming years.[3]

While robo-advisors are capable of allocating assets across the various asset classes and to different investment products (stocks, bonds, commodities, etc.), the funds are usually directed towards ETF portfolios because these provide a low-cost and index-based approach to investing in large chunks of the market. That said, through most robo-advisors, the investor can still choose between passive or active asset management techniques. Passive investing is where investors aim for minimal trading in the market and often use a buy-and-hold strategy with long-term investment horizons. Index investing is the most common form. Active investing implies ongoing buying and selling.

## Sustainable investment apps

Interestingly, many of the early robo-advisors still claim to be mission-driven in that their aim is to transform financial services to be more responsible to consumers. This is fantastic as democratisation of investing is a fundamental objective. The really exciting development has been how several robo-advisory firms have established sustainable investing or 'socially responsible' portfolios, and a number of targeted investment apps, tailored specifically to the sustainable investor, have begun to emerge.

As with robo-advisory platforms, targeted investment apps are making sustainable investing much easier and more accessible so that consumers like us can invest while also directing our funds towards specific outcomes and impact. The exciting thing about these targeted apps is that they are not only offering different investment choices, but at the same time providing educational support as well as regular market updates to help investors make more informed investment decisions.

## Blockchain

Blockchain technology (the record-keeping technology behind bitcoin) is actually easier to get your head around than you think. Blockchain allows for secure financial transactions to occur without the need for any third party. The implications of this are huge because it could essentially do away with financial institutions such as banks and investment managers.

Blockchain is pretty much literally a chain of blocks. However, these blocks comprise digital information and are stored in a public database, 'the chain'.

These blockchain technologies have the potential to revolutionise how we operate because of the way in which they can store, manage and transfer value between different digital identities. For example, blockchain tokens can be used to crowdfund innovative business concepts and make transaction-based processes much more efficient.

Of course, blockchain has made its way into the sustainable investing world and has many uses that can be taken advantage of to help build up the sector. For example, blockchain has supported the emergence of 'impact tokens', a value measure linked to a specific impact activity. Other advantages include:[4]

- Enhanced transparency – through its open-source and very nature, blockchain can improve the level of trust, a vital component of the sustainable investment market.

- Improved traceability and greater security – through better attribution and tracking of the impact of an investment, investors can trace where funds are going and have greater peace of mind over this.

- Increased efficiency and speed of transactions – blockchain allows for much faster and more efficient transitions, obviously accelerating the flow of investments, which can be a good thing for the sustainable investing world.

- Reduced costs – yes, once again, lower transaction costs lead to lower costs for the sustainable investor.

For certain, blockchain can have a profound impact on the sustainable investment world, in part through transforming the global payment (or transfer of value) system, but also through other aspects related to advancing sustainable development, such as supply chain management and access to finance. The implications are huge and can significantly enable our achievement of the SDGs – an ambition that many of us are serious about realising.

## Big data

Big data is massive amounts of structured and unstructured information. The field of big data looks at how to extract and analyse this information in a systematic way from data sets that are simply too complex or large to be managed by traditional data processing software. The reason why this is exciting for sustainable investing is because big data can be used to really understand the social and environmental impact of companies, in a much more accurate and comprehensive way.

With better data, investors can be more confident about the investment choices they are making and the impact or effects of these investments. We know that defective data and developments in the performance metrics for ESG have been two major factors preventing sustainable investment from going mainstream.[5] In itself, big data has the potential to transform this and build critical market confidence.

As with other technological advancements, certain factors are holding back big data's influence on the investment world – such as concerns about privacy, ensuring the correct use of data and a continued lack of, or limited, data.

An example of a company leveraging the developments of big data in the sustainable investing world is Arabesque, a global asset manager which uses self-learning quant models and big data to assess the performance and sustainability of globally listed companies. Arabesque claims to be processing over 100 billion data points via 250,000 lines of code to construct its investment strategies and approaches to stock selection.[6] Which is impressive.

## LET'S TAKE A LOOK AT WHO IS DOING WHAT

Over the last few years, there have been some exciting developments on the fintech front, and here I highlight just a few to have on your radar. If the market develops as many hope it will, we should see a number of innovative tech platforms crop up that help address the pressing need for sustainable investing options. Note – at the time of writing, these platforms are only available to investors in certain countries.

### Ellevest

Ellevest is probably one of the most widely known digital investment platforms specifically designed for US-based female investors – with the admirable goal of closing gender money gaps through modern, low-cost investing delivered via its simple and easy-to-use website and mobile app. Since Ellevest was publicly launched in 2016, co-founder and driving force Sallie Krawcheck has become a leading voice on the need to address the unique financial requirements of women.

In 2019, Ellevest announced it had closed its own $33 million funding round, bringing in some big-name investors to support the growth of the company. On closing the round, Ms Krawcheck put it brilliantly:

Today, we bring in a group of rock star investors deeply aligned with our mission. And it's no coincidence that many of them are unparalleled changemakers and advocates for women who understand that being under-invested can cost women a fortune over their lives. And it can be life-changing money. Retire-like-an-Instagram-influencer money. Get-your-hand-off-my-leg money.[7]

Given the burgeoning support, expect some big and exciting things from Ellevest. Its primary focus is on tapping into a large number of women who are looking for a low-cost way to start investing their money. It combines financial education with digital and varying degrees of human advice, so really provides flexibility and customisation depending on what women are looking for. For example, if you want just the digital offering it is priced at 0.25 per cent of assets under management. But it also offers more traditional wealth management services for clients with at least $1 million of investable assets.

The other interesting thing about Ellevest is its move into the impact investing space, in particular with the launch of Ellevest Intentional Impact Portfolios. On the private wealth management side, the Ellevest team has been working with clients to understand what it means for them to invest for impact for a while. The Intentional Impact Portfolios take this one step further – separately managed equity accounts that customise client holdings down to the individual company level.

Each company is evaluated on certain criteria developed by the team, all of which are about doing the right thing by women, or helping clients redirect their money away from companies with products, policies and practices that may harm them. These criteria include the more prominent issues like workplace diversity and labour relations, but also go deeper into the kind of issues that women contend with every day, across the world, including GHG emissions (because we know that climate change disproportionately affects women),[8] war, ethics and fraud. While only available to high-net-worth clients, it is a fantastic move in the right direction and sends some positive and strong signals to the market in terms of what female investors are wanting.

## Vested

Vested is an innovative impact assessment platform which essentially offers the investor the ability to understand and monitor the impact of their investments, and invest their money where it can make the most difference to solving the SDGs. I love the goal of Vested – to redefine the notion of a 'millionaire' to be a person who has impacted millions of lives. With the mission of enabling everyday investors, like you and me, to make their money work for them and the planet, it is worth checking out. Just one definitional point of note – Vested is focused on impact investing so prioritises those companies that have 'an intentional focus to create positive societal impact that would not otherwise occur'. This means it's not about choosing whether Facebook is more sustainable than Uber – that's a minimum baseline. It's about companies like Vestas – which builds wind farms – or ODDBOX – which distributes 'wonky' fruit and vegetables to avoid food waste. It is about doing good business.

What I particularly love about Vested is how it leverages technology to allow transparency and clarity for everyone. From the investor perspective, it makes it really easy – starting with as little as $100, you can track your personalised impact through Vested's proprietary impact measurement. This measurement uses a data-driven algorithm to trace, track and translate impact, integrating hundreds of thousands of leading bodies of standards, databases and metrics. It applies these to an asset's 'theory of change' in order to weight predicted and existing performance, translating it into a single, easy to understand and relevant measure of impact. How cool is that?

It is also using tech to do the legwork in building truly impact-focused portfolios and funds. Social change is interconnected: if we want to improve action on SDG 8 (Sustainable Economic Growth), we should be improving our efforts on SDG 5 (Achieving Gender Equality), as well as moving forward on SDG 10 (Reducing Inequalities). Vested calculates and maps the degree to which assets in a portfolio amplify, or hinder, the impact of one on another. The idea is that impact can be rebalanced and maximised according to what the investor cares most about. It's potentially the future 'social stock market'! One that will make money and make a difference.

## KIMBERLEY ABBOTT, FOUNDER AND CEO, VESTED

*Vested is a company with a mission to 'redefine millionaire to be a person who impacts millions of lives' through leveraging data-driven impact assessment to help people invest their money where it makes the best impact on society.*

**What inspired you to set up Vested? What are the core problems you are hoping to address in the investment market?**

The world is short an estimated $3 trillion a year to solve the Sustainable Development Goals. So, I realised if we are going to finance change, we need to change finance. Impact investing is one of the fastest-growing financial trends, with an estimated $25 trillion waiting to be invested. However, the key issue holding this 'world-changing money' back is that investors want to know where it will actually make a difference. For example, which companies will do the best with the capital? How do we hold these companies to account on impact? And on a more personal level, 'Did my money make a difference?' To address this, I developed the Vested algorithm to provide transparency so an investor knows their impact and can see where their money can make the most effective, biggest, or even local, impact.

**What role do the SDGs play in how Vested works? Can users directly link their investments to achievement of specific SDGs?**

The SDGs are the core anchor of the Vested algorithm. Everything is linked back to the SDGs, both because it provides a clear way to map data from our millions of data points, but also because there is no better guidepost for what we should be focusing on than the SDGs.

**How do you see the role of technology playing out in the sustainable investment industry in both the medium and long term? What are the big trends to watch?**

Big impact requires the contributions and empowerment of millions. Millions of users requires scale. And scale requires technology and systems to support. Technology provides us with a phenomenal opportunity to create things on a scale we have never seen. The most exciting thing is that most of the technology we need already exists.

I definitely feel in the next few years there will be a huge trend in leveraging digital technologies to regain trust in social impact and provide traceability, transparency and validation of impact. Technologies like machine learning, artificial intelligence and blockchain will come into play with these data systems and we will become smarter about how our money makes an impact and how we can be held accountable for it.

I am also fascinated by the 'simplification' of tech and the expansion of low-cost networks. As an engineer, we like to make things complex, but the trend of making things as simple as possible provides amazing opportunity, particularly across developing countries, by building platforms that can scale and reach millions of those who would not otherwise be reached. Ultimately in the long term, as the wonders of tech evolve, I believe it's the 'human' side that will become most important. I believe we will see impact investing become the norm, and the limiting factor will not be having enough 'good' to invest in – it will be the capacity of individuals to embrace a new form of wealth and to benefit from a new form of social contribution.

## OpenInvest

Some of the tech solutions we are seeing pop up have fantastic missions and OpenInvest's is certainly one of these – OpenInvest is 'dedicated to using technology to bring honesty and transparency to financial services, while making socially responsible investing accessible to everyone'.[9] Perfectly aligned with the purpose of this book!

OpenInvest was established in 2015. Its platform enables customisation, direct indexing and impact investing at scale for financial advisors, institutions and individual investors. OpenInvest helps investment advisors create personalised passive investment portfolios for every one of their clients. These portfolios are tailored to align with the issues their clients care about – gender equality, environmental sustainability, immigration reform, people with disabilities – or wish to avoid, such as tobacco products, gun or weapon manufacturers.

OpenInvest also has a simpler offering for individual investors, who can open accounts and invest with just $100. Because of this low minimum, it really has the potential to take sustainable investing to the masses (at least in the US). Technology has made this all possible: OpenInvest pulls in multi-sourced ESG data and integrates this into the investment offering. Investors can then identify a number of causes, such as divestment from fossil fuel companies, corporate leadership in gender diversity, LGBTQ-friendly companies, and so on, and have them integrated into their portfolio. The company's 'secret sauce' is to create portfolios that are passively managed, targeting similar performance, but with portfolio holdings that are aligned to the individual investor's values.

## CLAIRE VEUTHEY, FORMER DIRECTOR OF ESG AND IMPACT, OPENINVEST

*OpenInvest is a Registered Investment Advisor and Public Benefit Corporation leveraging technology to provide a next-generation impact investing solution.*

**Tell us more about how OpenInvest came about and how it is delivering on its mission for individual investors.**

The company was founded by two of the architects of Bridgewater Associates' portfolio management and trading systems and a sustainable finance expert from the World Wildlife Fund, with backing from Andreessen Horowitz, Y Combinator, Kevin Durant's Thirty Five Ventures and the founders of CapitalOne. Headquartered in San Francisco, OpenInvest now employs a staff of financial, technology and sustainability leaders across three continents, and is recognised as a global leader in ESG portfolio implementation.

OpenInvest's founders and team are passionate about using technology to make values-aligned investing more accessible. Through varied previous experiences working at hedge funds, in fintech, ESG investment firms and mission-driven organisations, we individually saw mounting evidence that we were not alone. Today's and tomorrow's investors care deeply about investing in ways that align with their own values. A 2017 study found 80 per cent of individual investors are interested in sustainable investments that can be customised to meet their interests and goals. A separate study, from 2018, found that 77 per cent of high-net-worth millennials currently own or are interested in impact investments.

So, OpenInvest set out to democratise impact investing. The platform allows anyone with $100 to open an account and create their own portfolio of investments that align with their values.

**Technology seems to be playing such a critical role in democratising access to sustainable investment options – how do you see this playing out over the next few years?**

We talk about a post-fund world, where mutual funds and electronically traded funds are no longer relevant. These investment vehicles deliver a one-size-fits-all approach to investing, removing a large measure of control of investment choice and shareholder engagement from the individual investor. Now, with platforms like OpenInvest that deliver capabilities such as dynamic custom indexing, investors or their advisors can construct customised portfolios that transfer more control over investment choices to the individual investor. For financial advisors, it allows them the benefits of mass customisation of investment portfolios at scale to address each client's specific goals, without compromising their fiduciary duty to their clients, or creating immense operational overhead. OpenInvest's tools help advisors create a more loyal and engaged client base and renew the concept of the trusted advisor.

## Sarwa

Fintech solutions aren't just happening in Europe and North America. For example, check out Sarwa, a Middle East-based automated investment platform that is rapidly gaining traction with young professionals in the region. Similar to other case studies here, Sarwa is a robo-advisor that leverages technology to deliver tailored investments for its clients' financial profiles, building diversified portfolios with low-cost ETFs and starting with low investment minimums.

Part of this tailoring and customisation includes Sarwa offering its clients, in addition to the usual conventional portfolios, Halal and 'Socially Responsible Investment' portfolios. This means that, as an investor, if you choose to select an SRI portfolio, you will be directed towards ETFs in the SRI space, hopefully limiting your exposure to companies that have a negative social impact while growing exposure to companies that have a positive one. While limited in sustainable investing ETF options, these include a number of BlackRock ETFs such as iShares MSCI KLD 400 Social ETF (including 'socially responsible' US companies, stocks that have been screened for ESG characteristics) and iShares ESG MSCI EAFE ETF (which accesses large- and mid-cap stocks in Europe, Australia, Asia and the Far East).

## Nutmeg

Nutmeg is one of the largest fintech companies in the UK and is all about digital wealth management for 'a much broader section of society who have less to invest and can start investing with us with as little as £100'.[10] As with other platforms, the aim is to democratise wealth management – and this also includes providing clients with sustainable investing options.

The investment team has a process for continuously scoring every portfolio using certain ESG principles, based on thousands of data points across key ESG issues. Nutmeg also works with MSCI to give each of the portfolios a range of ESG scores so that investors can get a good sense of how each portfolio aligns with their values.

## A FEW FINAL WORDS OF CAUTION

While technology is disrupting not only the financial industry but the way we invest sustainably, it is not without difficulties or certainly challenges to be aware of. There is much to be embraced but there are also a few final words of caution.

### Human advice still plays a critical role

Ultimately, robo-advisors cannot replace the human element of in-person advice and interaction. While this may not matter for some, there are still many in the industry who believe that the dominant model for wealth management will remain human advice – with technology as a facilitator and overlay.[11] Robo-advisors certainly are not for everyone – and, at this stage, it seems they are probably better suited to those who want digital-first, with less suitability for those with very complex financial situations.

### Struggle to gain customers

Some robo-advisory platforms and investment apps have failed to secure enough customers to ensure the ongoing sustainability of the businesses. Take, for example, Swell Investing – a US-based impact investing platform that allowed its customers to invest in portfolios of companies solving global challenges. Opened in 2017 with financial backing from Pacific Life, it closed its doors in August 2019 because of insufficient scale to sustain its operations.

Even for established platforms like Nutmeg there are limitations – only 40 per cent of Nutmeg's users are first-time investors. For sure, technology is lowering the bar to entry but, certainly at this point, tech solutions are not necessarily reaching the underserved majority.

## Passive investing

There is a lot of debate around whether passive investing and sustainability are incompatible, with some arguing that the two are irreconcilably different because sustainable investing requires making active decisions.[12] Much of this debate is occurring at the institutional investor level. For retail investors, the discussion is still relevant but, with technology allowing us to access both targeted investment platforms and ETFs, passive investing is supporting investors moving their assets towards sustainability options.

Some consider that individual stocks are a better way to construct a sustainable investment (or socially responsible) portfolio than with ETFs which are designed to filter out those that do not fit with the sustainability criteria. Both can be offered by robo-advisors and, of course, through human advisors!

## Customising tech solutions for women

We know that the investment industry is already grappling with how to better engage with its female client base. This is also relevant to how we build technology that is more female-friendly, requiring that these platforms are built with women in mind and by women. 'Digital empathy' is needed to ensure that female investors feel heard and represented, and that their digital experiences resonate with their needs.[13] The use of their data should also be leveraged to ensure that any predefined online persona is reflective of who they are and what they are looking for from their online experiences. In 2020, some fascinating research was published by the Financial Alliance for Women, which surveyed 168 fintechs and 30 investors and other ecosystem players from around the world. The report argues that fintechs 'have to move beyond building gender-neutral products, or simply changing the interface design and color to create a "female-friendly" variant of the same service if they want to tap into the women's market in a meaningful way'.[14]

## The need for due diligence

There is a great deal of hype around tech, as I am sure you know, and the recent hype around virtual currencies and tokens as a means to raise funds has brought with it its fair share of fraudulent activities, along with other concerns about the scope and reach of tech. With these concerns comes the call for more scrutiny and due diligence – all of which are highly relevant to the sustainable investing world. Ensuring the integrity of digital platforms and currencies is central to building the market confidence that is needed.

# THIRTEEN

## IT'S OVER TO YOU NOW

Our conversation is drawing to a close. But this is just the beginning of your personal sustainable investment journey. It is also the beginning of significant change in the financial industry as it embraces the economic, financial and moral imperative of sustainable investing. What's more, I like to believe it is the beginning of a massive shift in how we perceive the purpose of capital and understand the reasons behind why we invest. Because it is at this point in time that we must ask the question – and answer it – how do we reframe the role and remit of our financial systems so that these very systems can deliver real social and environmental benefits to the majority (and I mean the MAJORITY) of people?

Women stand at the heart of this new dawn – I know that, I see that, and I feel that every day. Many of my friends asked me about the title *Financial Feminism* and why I decided to run with this. Feminism isn't just one thing. It means different things to different people. To me, feminism represents a movement with a common goal

– and that goal is to create positive social, political and economic change that puts women front and centre, not marginalised or underrepresented.

At the beginning of this book I defined financial feminism as being financial equality for women. But I took this concept of financial equality one step further. It is not just about women earning and investing on a par with men. No. To me, financial feminism represents the opportunity for women to use their financial resources to drive positive change. Our voice can increasingly be heard in our financial power, as we shout loud and clear about the kind of world we want to live in and the kind of world we want to build for future generations.

I leave you with some final thoughts about where we go from here. First, as we look outwards, what is happening out there, beyond our individual choices, that may make a difference to the journey we take? And then as we look inwards, what can we do as individuals, how can we use the choices we have? I am issuing a 'call to action' because we don't want the conversation to stop here. We have so much work we can do together.


## WHERE NEXT FOR SUSTAINABLE INVESTING?

Sustainable investing is evolving at a rapid pace. In part because, collectively, we are waking up to the dire situation we are in when it comes to all things related to sustainability. It also happens that more people are joining the dots between their money, their wealth, and how they can use this to effect change in the world around them.

Even on a day-to-day basis, sustainable investment products are being launched, research and evidence rebuffing old-school myths are being published, the mainstream media is focusing its attention on some of our biggest concerns such as climate change and modern slavery. This was not happening ten years ago. Actually, it wasn't happening five years ago. So, looking forward, maybe five years or maybe ten years ahead, what are we to expect?

## Part of the bigger picture

The rapid growth in sustainable investing is highly likely to continue. We are seeing growing demand for sustainable investments, from all corners of the world, and we are seeing supply slowly start to expand as well. Given that our sustainability challenges aren't going away anytime soon, there is only really one direction this can move in, right?

Pardon the pun, but when it comes to money the penny is finally dropping. People, including women like you and me, are raising questions about their investment choices. We are thinking about how we can change these to reflect our personal values as well as our concern for the state of our world. At the same time, we now find that we have access to so much more information – information on companies, on corporate practices and on who is doing what. We also have access to tools and platforms that can make investing a whole lot easier and more democratic.

But it is also part of the much bigger picture. It is part of the broader consumer trends we are experiencing in other areas of our lives – think about, for example, the attention we now give to reducing our dependence on single-use plastic products. Or the efforts we make to buy food from local producers. Think about how we now talk about sustainable fashion and the number of high street names that are launching ethical product ranges. Think about the climate warriors who are forging ahead and demanding more from our global leaders. There is change afoot in all aspects of our lives.

## The role of governments and regulations

I will admit that I am a bit of a politico (I voluntarily chose to take a Master's degree in political theory, if that tells you anything) so I cannot let you escape without considering the role that our governments and our regulators can or should play.

On the positive side, in a number of countries we are finally seeing interest from governments and regulators on the importance of building financial systems and economies that reflect a sense of environmental and social responsibility in the corporate world. On the negative side, the actual policies and regulations are taking a long time to materialise and, in many instances, are not really going far enough. We need both carrots and sticks to drive the kind of behaviour that designs and delivers for a future-fit world.

Take, for example, environmental risk, which is now acknowledged as a key risk to global welfare and security.

Norms are changing quickly and thankfully we are seeing the green shoots of a long overdue transition to a lower-carbon society. Our national governments and global governing institutions have a responsibility to use policy and regulatory levers to ensure that this transition happens so that any losses – societal, human or economic – are kept to the absolute minimum.

Policy and regulation can be designed and implemented at different levels within a society. Done well, they can drive extensive change in the financial markets and the corporate sector. But they can also drive change at the level of the individual. As demand grows for sustainable investment products, policy makers and regulators can support the growth of the market through, for example, stronger incentives for the financial industry, greater transparency requirements so investors know what they are getting, and penalties for the negative externalities caused by companies we so easily turn a blind eye to. This has to be part of our collective future.

### It's the future – let's get on with it

There are now many in the financial industry who will tell you that ESG and sustainable investing is here to stay. Perhaps fewer people who will admit quite how much work the industry has to do to get us there.

One of the biggest roadblocks is the lack of standardisation – in particular, in terms of how things are labelled so that there is a common understanding across the board. Lack of standardisation is leading to a great deal of confusion among investors, both large institutions and individual retail investors. Sometimes it's just not clear what is what and the industry needs to sort this out as soon as possible, as it is holding people back from committing more capital.

The other worry, of course, is the issue of greenwashing, which is leading investors down the wrong path in some instances. Particularly for those of us who are relying on certain labels such as 'green' or 'SDGs' or 'gender diversity' to guide us in the right direction when we make an investment decision. The problem is that sometimes these labels are not properly assigned, or maybe misusing certain words to imply greater action is being taken than actually is the case. This gives the investor a false sense of comfort, not to mention the damage it does to the reputation of the sustainable investment industry.

Uptake and adoption of ESG by financial advisors has also been patchy. Some of the more old-school advisors still cite concerns about performance and track records, often still asking 'are investors actually interested?' The industry needs to figure out how to get over this hump because the financial advisor community stands to lose out big time, particularly with technology platforms biting at their heels.

So, the future is full of change, but this requires the financial industry to get its act together and solve some of the deeper issues it is currently avoiding. I suspect governments will step in to push this a little faster. Well, here's hoping so.

## The young are rising

Watching our youth lead from the front is perhaps one of the most beautiful and inspirational trends to emerge in these challenging times. From Greta Thunberg and her climate warriors to young social enterprise leaders seeking societal and equitable solutions, we have many reasons to be hopeful.

It turns out that younger generations are also really engaged with the idea of using their wealth to drive positive impact. There is quite a bit of research out there that confirms this trend. For example, a 2019 report from Morgan Stanley told us that, in the US, a staggering 95 per cent of millennial investors surveyed were interested in sustainable investing, with 67 per cent already adopters (the survey included individual investors with minimum investable assets of $100,000).[1] This is a big deal given the huge transfer of wealth to younger generations that is expected to occur. Again, in the US, a study shows that millennials will inherit over $68 trillion from their parents, holding five times as much wealth as they have today.

This is all good news and gives us so much hope for the future. Young people are rising, they are speaking their values loud and clear. They are using these values to guide decisions in all aspects of their lives, and they deserve our wholehearted support. I am hopeful that some readers of this book are not only women but also millennials and my words may be sowing the seeds of amazing things to come. If so, be brave, now is your time.

## MY CALL TO ACTION

While the future may look shiny for sustainable investing, we still have to take action today to get us to that glorious future. By now, I genuinely hope you feel empowered and motivated to do something with all that you have read over these pages. Act now.

### 1. Start with yourself

It is really simple – identify what your priorities are and get your sustainable investment strategy down on paper. Go back to Chapter 7 and actually do what I suggest. It really is the first step and will lead to a whole host of actions that you can then take.

Also, make the commitment to keep on learning. The world of sustainable investing is rapidly evolving, and that means there is an ever-increasing amount of data and research out there. If you don't want this to be all finance-related, make sure you are keeping on top of developments in the areas you are most concerned about, whether that be air pollution, access to healthcare, protection of the rainforests or whatever.

And don't stop asking questions. Ask questions of yourself, your colleagues, your family and of the investment professionals you choose to work with. This isn't the time to be shy or embarrassed about what you don't know. This is the time to get intellectually prepared.

## 2. Be part of the movement

I actually believe that being a sustainable investor is part of a bigger movement that is already starting to happen. We are questioning the role that our values should be playing and how we can stay true to these. This is happening as we think about money, wealth and investment and what this means for our society.

Be part of that movement, build, grow and recruit. Join an investment club, one that considers sustainability as a concern or priority. If you can't find one, why not start one of your own? Don't be scared – investment clubs are only really money-circles which can bring together like-minded women to share financial goals, ideas, ask questions and learn from one another. A co-learning space, if you like. Or even like a book club!

Find people to connect with and work together. With so many forums and initiatives popping up specifically targeting women and their relationship with money, get involved and make it your job to bring the sustainability discussion to the table. I have no doubt you will find a receptive audience.

## 3. Push the financial industry to do better

We have talked about generating demand for sustainable investment products and services quite a bit throughout the book. I urge you to help verbalise our demands to the financial industry so that all the players in it do a better job at addressing our needs – both as women and as sustainable investors.

That may be raising sustainable investment with your bank or your financial advisor, it may be contacting your pension fund to find out exactly what it's up to, it may be taking to social media to ask questions and share experiences. All of this helps push the financial industry in the right direction. We're asking its members to change their practices in ways that can spread sustainable investing even further. They should be doing more.

## 4. Shout out about sustainable investing

Talk to your friends and family about what you are thinking and doing on sustainable investing. Share the journey, not just the results – while results matter, the reasoning behind those results can be equally as powerful. Change needs to happen in others, not just yourself, so use your influence to support others in thinking differently about their money and their wealth.

In sharing, don't forget to zoom out to the bigger picture – changing how we invest is intrinsically linked to the change we want to see in the world around us. Always keep the bigger picture in mind because that is what our financial empowerment is all about – aiming not just for bigger, but for much, much better.

# NOTES

**PREFACE**

1.  In 2019, the *Financial Times* launched 'Moral Money' – 'news and analysis about the fast-expanding world of socially responsible business, sustainable finance, impact investing, environmental, social and governance (ESG) trends, and the UN's Sustainable Development Goals'. Read more at www.ft.com/moral-money


**ONE: MONEY, MONEY, MONEY – WOMEN AND THE THORNY ISSUE OF WEALTH**

1.  The World Economic Forum runs a project called Closing the Gender Gap, which aims to create national and global action platforms to address current and emerging economic gender gaps. The WEF's *Global Gender Gap Report 2020* concluded it would take 257 years to achieve global economic gender parity. Available at www3. weforum.org/docs/WEF_GGGR_2020.pdf

2.  Ellevest is a US-based robo-advisory service specifically designed for female investors. Its Mind the Gap Guide identifies and describes the different gender gaps that women may encounter. Available at production.assets.ellevest.com/documents/Ellevest-Mind-the-Gap-Guide.pdf

3.  There are different estimates of the gender pay gap, and this varies between countries. The International Labour Organization produces annual reports which provide real wages around the world, giving a picture of wage trends globally and by region. Available at www.ilo. org/wcmsp5/groups/public/---dgreports/---dcomm/---publ/documents/ publication/wcms_650553.pdf

4.  Kate Clark, 'US VC investment in female founders hits all-time high', *TechCrunch*, 9 December 2019, available at www.techcrunch. com/2019/12/09/us-vc-investment-in-female-founders-hits-all-time-high

5. Stephanie Lane, 'The scary facts behind the gender pension gap', World Economic Forum, 7 March 2018, available at www.weforum. org/agenda/2018/03/retired-women-less-money-pensions-than-men

6. Tim Cooper, 'It's time to tackle the gender pension gap', Raconteur, 31 January 2019, available at www.raconteur.net/hr/gender-pension-gap

7. Fidelity International, *The Financial Power of Women*, 2018, available at www.fidelity.co.uk/assets/pdf/personal-investor/markets-insights/women-and-money/fidelity-women-report.PDF

8. Laura Dew, 'Why are women losing out?', Money Management, 17 May 2019, available at www.moneymanagement.com.au/features/why-are-women-losing-out

9. Dan Moore, 'Gender investment gap estimated at £15bn', *FT Adviser*, 7 December 2018, available at www.ftadviser.com/investments/2018/12/07/gender-investment-gap-estimated-at-15bn

10. Jeffry Pilcher, 'Four myths banks believe about women consumers', The Financial Brand, 29 October 2014, available at www.the financialbrand.com/44420/four-myths-about-women-in-banking

11. Hilary Osborne, 'Why women need to stop saving their cash – and start investing', *Guardian*, 8 April 2019, available at www. theguardian.com/lifeandstyle/2019/apr/08/why-women-need-to-stop-saving-their-cash-and-start-investing

12. Godelieve van Dooren, 'The gender gap in retirement savings in ASEAN', Brink, 29 November 2018, available at www.brinknews. com/the-gender-gap-in-retirement-savings-in-asean

13. Tanya Jeffries, 'Women savers plan to retire on 168k, while men expect to build pots worth a quarter of a million', This is Money, 27 May 2019, available at www.thisismoney.co.uk/money/pensions/article-7067647/Women-savers-plan-retire-168k-men-expect-255k.html

14. Annalisa Esposito, 'What's stopping women from investing?', Morningstar, 9 October 2019, available at www.morningstar.co.uk/uk/news/196296/whats-stopping-women-from-investing.aspx

15. Starling Bank commissioned a linguistics study from semiotics and cultural value agency The Answer, which assessed 300 articles from a mix of outlets aimed at men and women. The research found that 65 per cent of articles define women as excessive spenders, advising them to limit shopping 'splurges', save small sums or depend on financial support. Seventy per cent of articles aimed at men emphasise that making money is a masculine ideal, and that monetary success and financial literacy are essential to enhancing personal status. Starling Bank has launched the #MAKEMONEYEQUAL campaign,

which calls for us to talk about money in the same way to everyone. Available at www.starlingbank.com/campaign/makemoneyequal

16. Wells Fargo Investment Institute, *Women and Investing: Building on Strengths*, January 2019, available at saf.wellsfargoadvisors.com/emx/dctm/Research/wfii/wfii_reports/Investment_Strategy/women_investing.pdf

17. Aegon, *Aegon's Investment Risk Index*, accessed in November 2019, available at www.aegon.co.uk/content/dam/ukpaw/documents/aegons-investment-risk-index.pdf

18. The term 'beating the benchmark' can be used to describe an investor (whether this be a fund manager or investment specialist) who produces a better-than-market-average return, using a benchmark (e.g. S&P 500 or Dow Jones Industrial Average Index) to measure performance against.

19. WealthiHer, *The WealthiHer Report 2019: Understanding the Diversity of Women's Wealth*, 2019, available at www.wealthihernetwork.com/report

20. Andrea Hasler and Annamaria Lusardi, *The Gender Gap in Financial Literacy: A Global Perspective*, Global Financial Literacy Excellence Center, July 2017, available at gflec.org/wp-content/uploads/2017/07/The-Gender-Gap-in-Financial-Literacy-A-Global-Perspective-Report.pdf?x87657

21. Laith Khalaf, 'Women who invest tend to outperform men', Hargreaves Lansdown, 6 February 2018, available at www.hl.co.uk/about-us/press/press-releases/women-who-invest-tend-to-outperform-men

22. Analysis carried out by Neil Stewart, Professor of Behavioural Science, Warwick Business School, compared male and female investors through Barclays and their trading behaviour over a 36-month period. While annual returns on investments for men were on average a marginal 0.14 per cent above the performance of the FTSE 100, annual returns on the investment portfolios held by women were 1.94 per cent above it. This means returns for women investing outperformed men by 1.8 per cent. 'Are women better investors than men?', Warwick Business School, 28 June 2018, available at www.wbs.ac.uk/news/are-women-better-investors-than-men

23. Fidelity Investments conducted a survey in 2016, *Who's the Better Investor: Men or Women?*. 'Results of this survey are based on an online omnibus conducted among a demographically representative US sample of 2,995 adults comprising 1,496 men and 1,499 women 18 years of age and older.' Fidelity Investments, 'Fidelity Investments

survey reveals only nine percent of women think they make better investors than men, despite growing evidence to the contrary', 18 May 2017, available at www.fidelity.com/about-fidelity/individual-investing/better-investor-men-or-women

24.  EY, *Women and Wealth: The Case for a Customized Approach*, accessed in November 2019, available at www.ey.com/Publication/vwLUAssets/EY-women-investors/$FILE/EY-women-and-wealth.pdf

25.  Caroline Cohn and Lawrence White, 'Major UK financial firms make little progress on gender pay gap', Reuters, 5 April 2019, available at uk.reuters.com/article/us-britain-gender-pay-finance-analysis/major-uk-financial-firms-make-little-progress-on-gender-pay-gap-idUKKCN1RH0Z5

26.  Jessica Clempner, Elizabeth St-Onge, et al., 'Serving women as financial services customers: Women in financial services 2020', Oliver Wyman, available at www.oliverwyman.com/our-expertise/insights/2019/nov/women-as-financial-services-customers.html

27.  This data is taken from 20-first's 'Global Gender Balance Scorecard 2018' – the data for this survey was based on information provided by companies listed in the 2017 Fortune Global 500. Data is taken from websites and annual reports, as of February 2018. Available at 20-first.com/wp-content/uploads/2018/09/2018-Scorecard_Financial-Services.pdf

28.  Morningstar has studied where women have made progress or retreated in the fund management industry. Laura Lallos, 'Women in investing: Morningstar's view, Morningstar, 2 March 2020, available at www.morningstar.com/articles/967691/women-in-investing-morningstars-view

29.  Richard Partington, '"If it was Lehman Sisters, it would be a different world" – Christine Lagarde', *Guardian*, 5 September 2018, available at www.theguardian.com/business/2018/sep/05/if-it-was-lehman-sisters-it-would-be-a-different-world-christine-lagarde

30.  Ratna Sahay and Martin Cihak, *Women in Finance: A Case for Closing Gaps*, International Monetary Fund – Staff Discussion Notes, 17 September 2018, available at www.imf.org/en/Publications/Staff-Discussion-Notes/Issues/2018/09/17/women-in-finance-a-case-for-closing-gaps-45136

## TWO: ENOUGH ALREADY – IT'S TIME FOR CHANGE

1.  Credit Suisse, *Why Wealth Matters: The Global Wealth Report*, 2020, available at www.credit-suisse.com/about-us/en/reports-research/global-wealth-report.html

2. Data from UNICEF published in October 2019 states that in the world's poorest countries slightly more than one in four children are engaged in child labour. Available at data.unicef.org/topic/child-protection/child-labour

3. 'Fast facts: 10 facts illustrating why we must #EndChildMarriage', UNICEF, 11 February 2019, available at www.unicef.org/eca/press-releases/fast-facts-10-facts-illustrating-why-we-must-endchildmarriage

4. Data taken from Sustainable Development Goal 5 – achieve gender equality and empower all women and girls. This was reported under 'Progress of Goal 5 in 2019', available at sustainabledevelopment.un.org/sdg5

5. UN Environment, *Global Environment Outlook 6 – Healthy Planet, Healthy People*, March 2019, available at www.unenvironment.org/resources/global-environment-outlook-6

6. 'A world of waste', The World Counts, accessed November 2019, available at www.theworldcounts.com/counters/shocking_environmental_facts_and_statistics/world_waste_facts

7. Mary Halton, 'Climate changes "impacts women more than men"', BBC News, 8 March 2018, available at www.bbc.com/news/science-environment-43294221

8. Podcast with impact investing pioneer Antony Bugg-Levine and IIX's Durreen Shahnaz: 'Impact investing's "Third Phase": What new challenges lie ahead?', Knowledge@Wharton, 27 June 2019, available at knowledge.wharton.upenn.edu/article/whats-next-for-impact-investing

9. Brent Beardsley, Bruce Holley, et al., 'Global wealth 2016: navigating the new client landscape', BCG, 15 June 2016, available at www.bcg.com/publications/2016/financial-institutions-consumer-insight-global-wealth-2016.aspx

10. EY, *Harnessing the Power of Women Investors in Wealth Management: A Look at the North American Market*, available at www.ey.com/Publication/vwLUAssets/ey-women-investors-in-wealth-management/$FILE/ey-women-investors-in-wealth-management.pdf

11. John Collett, 'Women closing the gap with men in wealth stakes', *Sydney Morning Herald*, 14 July 2019, available at www.smh.com.au/money/planning-and-budgeting/women-closing-the-gap-with-men-in-wealth-stakes-20190711-p52695.html

12. Lucy Warwick-Ching, 'Wealth managers adapt to appeal to female clients', *Financial Times*, 23 May 2019, available at www.ft.com/content/585cc928-764d-11e9-bbad-7c18c0ea0201

13. Morgan Stanley Institute for Sustainable Investing, *Sustainable Signals: New Data from the Individual Investor*, 2017, available at www.morganstanley.com/pub/content/dam/msdotcom/ideas/ sustainable-signals/pdf/Sustainable_Signals_Whitepaper.pdf

14. Lynne Ford, 'Why women and millennials are likely to drive growth in responsible investing', Green Money, April 2016, available at www.greenmoney.com/why-women-and-millennials-are-likely-to-drive-growth-in-responsible-investing

## THREE: WELCOME TO THE WONDERFUL WORLD OF INVESTING – COVERING OFF THE BASICS

1. In classical economics, capital is one of the four factors of production, the others being land, labour and organisation.

2. An investor makes a 'profit' or a financial gain when he or she sells the asset for a higher price than it was bought for, taking into account any transaction costs.

3. If you are struggling with the concept of compound interest, there are some useful explanations online. For example, Investopedia includes an explanatory video and illustrative calculations: www.investopedia.com/terms/c/compoundinterest.asp

4. J. B. Maverick, 'What is the average annual return for the S&P 500?', Investopedia, 19 February 2020, available at www.investopedia.com/ask/answers/042415/what-average-annual-return-sp-500.asp

5. A bear market is when share prices are falling, usually from recent highs, due to strong negative investor sentiment and widespread pessimism. Typically, the term is used when there are overall market declines or index drops (of 20 per cent or more, over a sustained period), but it can also be used when individual stocks fall in value. A bear market is in contrast to a bull market, which occurs when share prices are rising and there is strong expectation that these rises will continue. This encourages investors to buy securities with the expectation that the value of the shares will rise in the short term.

6. Brian Livingston, 'How low will the S&P 500 go? Buffett and Shiller know', Marketwatch, 9 March 2019, available at www.marketwatch.com/story/how-low-will-the-sp-500-go-buffett-and-shiller-know-2019-01-23

7. ETFs can provide the investor with exposure to all asset classes in a cost-effective manner. ETFs can be found in equities, bonds, commodities, real estate and money markets.

8. By way of example, 'the British Private Equity & Venture Capital Association calculates that, over the decade to 2013, its member funds generated an annual return rate of 15.7 per cent, compared with 8.8 per cent for the FTSE All-Share index. The average obscures a wide range of outcomes, and even well-established firms can have disastrous funds, complicating investors' selection process.' Stephen Foley, 'Private equity begins to entice ordinary investors', *Financial Times*, 26 May 2015, available at www.ft.com/content/e85240c4-b150-11e4-831b-00144feab7de

9. Ritoban Chakrabarti, '#9 out of 10 start-ups fail. Here's why!', Entrepreneur India, 14 June 2017, available at www.entrepreneur. com/article/295798

10. For a deeper discussion on the purpose of capital, you may be interested to look at the recent work of the renowned Jed Emerson. In his book *The Purpose of Capital: Elements of Impact, Financial Flows, and Natural Being,* Emerson looks at the underpinnings of our relationship to capital and its purpose in forwarding humanity in a living, thriving world. Read more at www.purposeofcapital.org

## FOUR: WHEN 'SUSTAINABLE INVESTING' BECOMES JUST 'INVESTING'

1. 'Sustainable investing basics', US SIF, accessed in November 2019, available at www.ussif.org/sribasics

2. The Global Sustainable Investment Alliance (GSIA) identifies the following sustainable investment activities and strategies. All or some may be used by institutional investors: 1. Negative/exclusionary screening; 2. Positive/best-in-class screening; 3. Norms-based screening; 4. ESG integration; 5. Sustainability-themed investing; 6. Impact/community investing; and 7. Corporate engagement and shareholder action. In 2018, 'the largest sustainable investment strategy globally is negative/exclusionary screening ($19.8 trillion), followed by ESG integration ($17.5 trillion) and corporate engagement/shareholder action ($9.8 trillion). Negative screening remains the largest strategy in Europe, while ESG integration continues to dominate in the United States, Canada, Australia and New Zealand in asset-weighted terms. Corporate engagement and shareholder action is the dominant strategy in Japan.' Global Sustainable Investment Alliance, *2018 Global Sustainable Investment Review,* available at www.gsi-alliance.org/wp-content/ uploads/2019/03/GSIR_Review2018.3.28.pdf

3. Institutional investors have increasingly used shareholder proposals to exert pressure on companies on certain ESG issues. For example, Ceres, the US-based non-profit sustainability advocacy organisation, identified that: 'Between 2011–2017, 51 shareholder proposals were filed by US investors asking for corporate policies to address financially material reputational and market risks associated with the sourcing of unsustainable palm oil and other deforestation-linked commodities.' *The Role of Investors in Supporting Better Corporate ESG Performance*, available at www.ceres.org/sites/default/files/reports/2019-04/Investor_Influence_report.pdf

4. The Rockefeller Foundation is well known for its support for the growth in the impact investing field. A long-time supporter of 'innovations that seek to catalyse private sector investment for social and environmental good', it is claimed that the term 'impact investing' was coined at the Rockefeller's Bellagio Center in Italy in 2007. Since that date the Foundation has continued to actively support organisations that are pushing for impact investing to take hold. Read more at www.rockefellerfoundation.org

5. Tracy Mayor, 'Impact investing is hot right now. Here's why.', MIT Management Sloan School, 17 September 2019, available at mitsloan.mit.edu/ideas-made-to-matter/impact-investing-hot-right-now-heres-why

6. Global Impact Investing Network, 'What you need to know about impact investing', available at www.thegiin.org/impact-investing/need-to-know/#what-is-impact-investing

7. Yossi Cadan, Ahmed Mokgopo and Clara Vondrich, '$11 trillion and counting', 350.org, September 2019, available at financingthefuture.platform350.org/wp-content/uploads/sites/60/2019/09/FF_11Trillion-WEB.pdf

8. Lorenzo Saa, 'PRI welcomes 500th asset owner signatory', PRI, 27 January 2020, available at www.unpri.org/pri-blog/pri-welcomes-500th-asset-owner-signatory/5367.article

9. Global Sustainable Investment Alliance, *Global Sustainable Investment Review 2018*, available at www.gsi-alliance.org/trends-report-2018

10. Eurosif, *European SRI Study 2018*, available at www.eurosif.org/wp-content/uploads/2018/11/European-SRI-2018-Study.pdf

11. Ray Sin and Samantha Lamas, 'Are your clients ESG investors?', Morningstar, 22 April 2019, available at www.morningstar.com/blog/2019/04/22/esg-investors.html

12. Jon Hale, 'The number of funds considering ESG explodes in 2019', Morningstar, 30 March 2020, available at www.morningstar.com/articles/973432/the-number-of-funds-considering-esg-explodes-in-2019

13. Chris Flood, 'Record sums deployed into sustainable investment funds', *Financial Times*, 20 January 2020, available at www.ft.com/content/2a6c38f7-4e4b-411b-b5e6-96b36e597cfc

14. Morgan Stanley Institute for Sustainable Investing, *Sustainable Reality: Analyzing Risk and Returns of Sustainable Funds*, 2019, available at www.morganstanley.com/pub/content/dam/msdotcom/ideas/sustainable-investing-offers-financial-performance-lowered-risk/Sustainable_Reality_Analyzing_Risk_and_Returns_of_Sustainable_Funds.pdf

15. Gunnar Friede, Timo Busch and Alexander Bassen, 'ESG and financial performance: aggregated evidence from more than 2000 empirical studies', *Journal of Sustainable Finance and Investment*, 5:4, 210–33, 2015, available at www.db.com/newsroom_news/2016/ghp/esg-and-financial-performance-aggregated-evidence-from-more-than-200-empirical-studies-en-11363.htm

16. Willis Owen reported: 'Ethical equity indices have beaten their mainstream peers in the UK and US over 1, 3, 5 and 10 years. To 3 October 2019 the ethical FTSE4GOOD index was up around 1%, whilst the main FTSE All Share index was actually down the same amount. Over ten years the gap has widened with the ethical index returning 125% compared to 118% for the FTSE All Share. The picture is the same in US, not a country renowned for its ethical approach. The S&P 500 has returned 321% over the same 10 year period (to 3 October 2019) whilst the comparable FTSE4Good US delivered a 373% return.' Adrian Lowcock, 'Good money week – ethical investing has outperformed the market', Willis Owen, 11 October 2019, available at www.willisowen.co.uk/insights/insight-article?Title=Good-Money-Week---Ethical-investing-has-outperformed-the-market&ID=438

17. Morningstar, *How Does European Sustainable Funds' Performance Measure Up?*, available at www.morningstar.com/en-uk/lp/European-Sustainable-Funds-Performance

18. Gloria Nelund and Joan Trant, 'Creating and distributing impact products for retail investors', Chapter 4.2 in *From Ideas to Practice, Pilots to Strategy II*, World Economic Forum Investors Industries, September 2014, available at reports.weforum.org/impact-investing-from-ideas-to-practice-pilots-to-strategy-ii/4-democratizing-impact-investing-for-retail-investors/4-2-creating-and-distributing-impact-

products-for-retail-investors/?doing_wp_cron=1552908368.14649701
11846923828125

19.  Gillian Tett, 'Does capitalism need saving from itself?', *Financial Times*, 6 September 2019, available at www.ft.com/content/b35342fe-cda4-11e9-99a4-b5ded7a7fe3f

## FIVE: CHECKING OUT THE SCENE – WHAT IS OUT THERE?

1.   Adam Connaker and Saadia Madsbjerg, 'The state of socially responsible investing', *Harvard Business Review*, 17 January 2019, available at hbr.org/2019/01/the-state-of-socially-responsible-investing

2.   S-Ray from Arabesque Partners is worth exploring. Anyone can use and access S-Ray, so it allows the everyday user to process and make sense of the huge amount of sustainability information that is out there. The idea is to empower users to feel that they can seek out companies that are aligned to their values. Take a look at Arabesque's S-Ray website – there is a free version, but you will have to create a log in, or you can do so through your LinkedIn account: sray.arabesque.com

3.   Samuel Chin, 'Stanchart flies sustainable-investing flag', *Business Times*, 13 June 2019, available at www.businesstimes.com.sg/life-culture/stanchart-flies-sustainable-investing-flag

4.   As a further interesting example, Standard Chartered Bank launched Asia's first Sustainable Deposit. It was launched to European investors in May 2019, and then extended to corporate and retail investors in Singapore, Hong Kong and New York later in the year. The funds raised are used to finance activities that support the SDGs in countries in Asia, Africa and the Middle East. Read more at www.sc.com/en/media/press-release/standard-chartered-singapore-launches-asias-first-sustainable-deposit

5.   The RI Marketplace was set up to make it easier and more accessible for investors to find suitable responsible investment products, services and advice. Take a look at the website to learn more about the listings: www.riacanada.ca/ri-marketplace

6.   MSCI, 'MSCI makes public ESG metrics for indexes and funds to drive greater ESG transparency', 20 May 2020, available at www.msci.com/documents/10199/c09b9fbb-faaf-0d56-bd08-342b540b690d

7.   If you want to learn more about ESG investing and bond portfolio investing, take a look at Barclays' report, *The Positive Impact of ESG*

*on Bond Performance* 31 October 2016, available at
www.investmentbank.barclays.com/our-insights/esg-sustainable-
investing-and-bond-returns.html#tab2

8.  BlackRock, 'BlackRock takes sustainable investing mainstream with
    range of low-cost sustainable core ETFs', 23 October 2018, available
    at ir.blackrock.com/file/Index?KeyFile=395440107

9.  The discussion paper identifies a few of the issues associated with
    the development of this market. PRI, *How Can a Passive Investor
    Be a Responsible Investor?*, 2019, available at www.unpri.org/
    download?ac=6729

## SIX: A GLOBAL CALL TO ACTION – INTRODUCING THE SUSTAINABLE DEVELOPMENT GOALS

1.  The Sustainable Development Goals Knowledge Platform provides
    a wealth of information – including details on the SDGs, additional
    resources and topic-specific analysis. There is also a whole host
    of information on the political process that sits behind the SDGs,
    partnerships and upcoming events. United Nations, 'The 17 goals',
    available at sustainabledevelopment.un.org/?menu=1300

2.  The SDGs evolved from the valuable lessons and experience gained
    from the MDGs. While progress had been made, it was clear that
    the job remained unfinished and the SDGs set out a more ambitious
    framework. UNDP, 'Sustainable development goals', available at
    www.undp.org/content/undp/en/home/sustainable-development-goals/
    background.html

3.  If you really want to get into the details, you can look at the 232
    indicators that sit under the 169 targets. These were agreed in
    March 2017 and form the global indicator framework. UN Stats,
    'SDG indicators', available at unstats.un.org/sdgs/indicators/
    indicators-list

4.  SDG 5 is based on the premise that: 'Gender equality is not only a
    fundamental human right, but a necessary foundation for a peaceful,
    prosperous and sustainable world.' UN, 'Goal 5: Achieve gender
    equality and empower all women and girls', available at www.un.org/
    sustainabledevelopment/gender-equality

5.  Women Deliver is a global advocacy organisation that champions
    gender equality and the health and rights of girls and women.
    Check out Women Deliver's website for some startling statistics on
    the benefits of women's economic empowerment. For example, if

another 600 million women had access to the internet, annual gross domestic product could increase by as much as $18 billion across 144 developing countries. Women Deliver, 'Women's economic empowerment is a pre-requisite for inclusive and equitable economic growth', available at womendeliver.org/investment/boost-womens-economic-empowerment

6. For some interesting analysis on what companies and industries are doing on SDGs along with case studies, read PwC's report published in 2018, *From Promise to Reality: Does Business Really Care About the SDGs?*, available at www.pwc.com/gx/en/sustainability/SDG/sdg-reporting-2018.pdf

7. United Nations Global Impact, 'Leadership for the decade of action', available at www.unglobalcompact.org

8. The SDG Gender Index (created by Equal Measures 2030) found that the global average score for the 129 countries indexed is 65.7 out of 100. This rates as 'poor' on the index scoring system. Equal Measures 2030, *2019 Global Report*, available at data.em2030.org/2019-global-report. 'With just 11 years to go, our index finds that not a single one of the 129 countries is fully transforming their laws, policies or public budget decisions on the scale needed to reach gender equality by 2030. We are failing to deliver on the promises of gender equality for literally billions of girls and women,' said Alison Holder, director of Equal Measures 2030, available at www.fortune.com/2019/06/05/sdg-gender-index-gender-equality

9. Tribe, *Tribe: Our Story So Far. Impact Report 2018–2019*, available at www.tribeimpactcapital.com/wp-content/uploads/Tribe_Impact_Report2018_2019.pdf

## SEVEN: DON'T BE PUT OFF – THE TIME IS NOW

1. Moxie Future – an information, community and blog platform that I set up to engage with women on sustainable investing issues – includes 'Your Responsible Investment Roadmap'. If you want more detailed and step-by-step guidance, check out moxiefuture.com/toolkit/your-responsible-investment-roadmap

2. Every year the UK Sustainable Investment and Finance Association (UKSIF) coordinates Good Money Week, aimed at raising awareness of sustainable, responsible and ethical finance – banking, pensions, savings and investments – to help people make good money choices. In 2019, Good Money Week included the #MENTIONTHEPENSION campaign – encouraging people to

'push for your pension savings to be used for "good" in the world by emailing your employer, pension provider or both. If enough of us speak up, we can help shape a pensions industry that finances a clean, stable, sustainable and prosperous future.' Read more at www.goodmoneyweek.com/pensions

3. Read more about the Statement on the Purpose of a Corporation at opportunity.businessroundtable.org/ourcommitment

4. Make My Money Matter, 'Pensions with intention', available at makemymoneymatter.co.uk

## EIGHT: IT IS NOT PLAIN SAILING

1. Cambridge Institute for Sustainability Leadership developed 'The Investment Impact Framework', which aims to enable a 'revolution' in consumer choice in financial services. 'The new framework meshes directly with the United Nations Sustainable Development Goals (SDGs) and aims to assist investors in understanding the alignment of their portfolios with the commitments of 193 countries, through six impact themes (basic needs, climate stability, decent work, healthy ecosystems, resource security and wellbeing). The new set of impact metrics is designed to translate the SDGs into measurable indicators that can be calculable, easily understood, and implementable by investors. The University of Cambridge seeks to provide robustness to the model and these metrics could be a guideline for the industry.' Cambridge Institute for Sustainability Leadership, 'Measuring investment impacts', available at www.cisl.cam.ac.uk/business-action/sustainable-finance/investment-leaders-group/measuring-investment-impacts

2. Read more at iris.thegiin.org

3. Read more at b-analytics.net/giirs-funds

4. Read more at navigator.sasb.org/#about

## NINE: IT CAN BE DONE – HERE'S HOW

1. 'The Paris Agreement's central aim is to strengthen the global response to the threat of climate change by keeping a global temperature rise this century well below 2 degrees Celsius above pre-industrial levels and to pursue efforts to limit the temperature increase even further to 1.5 degrees Celsius. Additionally, the agreement aims to strengthen the ability of countries to deal with the impacts of

climate change. To reach these ambitious goals, appropriate financial flows, a new technology framework and an enhanced capacity building framework will be put in place, thus supporting action by developing countries and the most vulnerable countries, in line with their own national objectives. The Agreement also provides for enhanced transparency of action and support through a more robust transparency framework.' For further information about the Paris Agreement, the underlying process and the commitments made, read United Nations, 'The Paris Agreement', available at unfccc.int/process-and-meetings/the-paris-agreement/the-paris-agreement

2. IPCC, *Summary for Policymakers of IPCC Special Report on Global Warming of 1.5°C Approved by Governments*, 8 October 2018, available at www.ipcc.ch/2018/10/08/summary-for-policymakers-of-ipcc-special-report-on-global-warming-of-1-5c-approved-by-governments

3. Jonathan Watts, 'We have 12 years to limit climate change catastrophe, warns UN', *Guardian*, 8 October 2018, available at www.theguardian.com/environment/2018/oct/08/global-warming-must-not-exceed-15c-warns-landmark-un-report

4. For further information on the concept and different types of stranding, read more on Carbon Tracker's website: www.carbontracker.org/terms/stranded-assets

5. Olivia Gagan, 'Should investors be wary of stranded assets?', Raconteur, 21 March 2019, available at www.raconteur.net/business-innovation/stranded-assets

6. Al Gore, 'The climate crisis is the battle of our time, and we can win', *New York Times*, 20 September 2019, available at www.nytimes.com/2019/09/20/opinion/al-gore-climate-change.html

7. US SIF, *Investing to Curb Climate Change: A Guide for the Individual Investor*, 2018, available at www.ussif.org/files/Publications/SRI_Climate_Guide.pdf

8. Read more at www.asyousow.org

9. Read more at www.fossilfreefunds.org

10. Read more at www.fsb-tcfd.org

11. US SIF has compiled the Mutual Fund and ETF Performance Chart, displaying all sustainable, responsible and impact mutual funds and ETFs offered by US SIF's institutional member firms. This public tool is meant for individual investors to compare cost, financial performance, screens and voting records of competing funds. All listed funds are open to new investors. Read more at charts.ussif.org/mfpc

12. Fiona Reynolds, 'Climate change will have an impact on all retail investors', *FT Adviser*, 5 December 2018, available at www.ftadviser.com/investments/2018/12/05/climate-change-will-have-an-impact-on-all-retail-investors/?page=1

13. Phillip Inman, 'Corporations told to draw up climate rules or have them imposed', *Guardian*, 8 October 2019, available at www.theguardian.com/business/2019/oct/08/corporations-told-to-draw-up-climate-rules-or-have-them-imposed

14. FashionUnited, 'Global fashion industry statistics – International apparel', available at fashionunited.com/global-fashion-industry-statistics

15. The World Bank, 'How much do our wardrobes cost the environment?', 23 September 2019, available at www.worldbank.org/en/news/feature/2019/09/23/costo-moda-medio-ambiente

16. UNICEF, 'Factsheet: child Labour', available at www.unicef.org/protection/files/child_labour.pdf

17. 'The fashion industry has a disastrous impact on the environment. In fact, it is the second largest polluter in the world, just after the oil industry. And the environmental damage is increasing as the industry grows.' Sustain Your Style, 'The fashion industry is the second largest polluter in the world', available at www.sustainyourstyle.org/old-environmental-impacts

18. Ellen MacArthur Foundation, *A New Textiles Economy: Redesigning Fashion's Future*, available at www.ellenmacarthurfoundation.org/assets/downloads/publications/A-New-Textiles-Economy_Full-Report_Updated_1-12-17.pdf

19. 'Burberry burns bags, clothes and perfume worth millions', BBC News, 19 July 2018, available at www.bbc.com/news/business-44885983

20. Vivian Hendriksz, 'H&M hit with fresh accusations over incinerating new clothes', FashionUnited, 23 November 2017, available at fashionunited.uk/news/fashion/h-m-hit-with-fresh-accusations-over-incinerating-new-clothes/2017112326944

21. Javier Seara, Sebastian Boger, et al., 'Sustainability is good business for fashion', BCG, 22 May 2018, available at www.bcg.com/en-mideast/publications/2018/sustainability-good-business-fashion.aspx

22. 'The *Pulse of the Fashion Industry* report is published by the Global Fashion Agenda, in collaboration with Boston Consulting Group and Sustainable Apparel Coalition. It follows the strong belief that the environmental, social and ethical challenges the industry faces today are not simply a threat, but instead an immense untapped value

creation opportunity.' To read more and download the report, go to: www.globalfashionagenda.com/initiatives/pulse/#

23. FashionUnited, 'Top 100 fashion companies index', available at fashionunited.com/i/top100

24. Kickstarter, 'Healthy, sustainable clothing', available at www.kickstarter.com/projects/803142011/healthy-sustainable-clothing

25. Read more at www.nextchaptercrowdfunding.com

## TEN: SISTERS DOING IT FOR THEMSELVES — GENDER-SMART INVESTING

1. Read more at www.catalystatlarge.com

2. Suzanne Biegel is the founder of Catalyst at Large and a global leader in gender-smart investing. Her mission is to 'increase the flow of global capital to gender-smart investments and initiatives, to make sure this capital is used in ways that will generate the most impact'. Read more at www.catalystatlarge.com/about

3. There are different takes on what gender-smart investing represents, and nuanced definitions on investing with a gender lens. For the purpose of this book, I refer to Catalyst at Large to define the different ways in which gender-smart investing opportunities can be realised as I believe it covers these succinctly. Catalyst at Large, 'What is gender-smart investing?', available at www.catalystatlarge.com/what-is-gendersmart-investing

4. The Global Impact Investing Network hosted the Gender Lens Investing Initiative and there are some useful resources on the website. The GIIN defines gender-lens investing in two broad categories: 1) investing with the intent to address gender issues or promote gender equity; 2) and/or investing with a gender approach or a gender strategy to inform investment decisions. Read more at thegiin.org/gender-lens-investing-initiative

5. Suzanne Biegel, Sandra M. Hunt and Sherryl Kuhlman, *Project Sage: Tracking Venture Capital With a Gender Lens*, Wharton University of Pennsylvania Social Impact Initiative, October 2017, available at socialimpact.wharton.upenn.edu/wp-content/uploads/2017/10/ProjectSageReport102317.pdf

6. For further information on the key takeaways from Project Sage 3.0, visit socialimpact.wharton.upenn.edu/research-reports/reports-2/project-sage-3

7.  Patricia Farrar-Rivas and Alison Pyott, 'Gender lens investing: assets grow to more than $3.4 billion', Veris, 4 March 2020, available at www.veriswp.com/gender-lens-investing-assets-grow-to-more-than-3-4-billion

8.  PitchBook, 'The VC female founders dashboard', last updated 6 July 2020; data through 30 June 2020, available at www.pitchbook.com/news/articles/the-vc-female-founders-dashboard

9.  Priyamvada Mathur, 'Quarterly VC funding for female founders drops to three-year low', PitchBook, 8 October 2020, available at www.pitchbook.com/news/articles/vc-funding-female-founders-drops-low

10. Pedro Gonçalves, 'Over a third of women entrepreneurs face gender bias when raising capital: HSBC', International Investment, 21 October 2019, available at www.internationalinvestment.net/news/4006112/women-entrepreneurs-gender-bias-raising-capital-hsbc

11. 'A "best in region" scenario in which all countries match the rate of improvement of the fastest-improving country in their region could add as much as $12 trillion, or 11 percent, in annual 2025 GDP. In a "full potential" scenario in which women play an identical role in labour markets to that of men, as much as $28 trillion, or 26 percent, could be added to global annual GDP by 2025.' Jonathan Woetzel, Anu Madgavkar, et al., 'How advancing women's equality can add $12 trillion to global growth', McKinsey Global Institute, September 2015, available at www.mckinsey.com/featured-insights/employment-and-growth/how-advancing-womens-equality-can-add-12-trillion-to-global-growth

12. Larry Elliott, 'More women in the workplace could boost economy by 35%, says Christine Lagarde', *Guardian*, 1 March 2019, available at www.theguardian.com/world/2019/mar/01/more-women-in-the-workplace-could-boost-economy-by-35-says-christine

13. Larry Fink, BlackRock's Chief Executive, writes an annual open letter to CEOs. It is widely read and hotly debated. In 2017, Fink chose to highlight the importance of diversity in boards. Larry Fink, 'A fundamental reshaping of finance', BlackRock, available at www.blackrock.com/hk/en/insights/larry-fink-ceo-letter

14. Meggin Thwing Eastman, Damion Rallis and Gaia Mazzucchelli, *The Tipping Point: Women on Boards and Financial Performance*, MSCI, December 2016, available at www.msci.com/documents/10199/fd1f8228-cc07-4789-acee-3f9ed97ee8bb

15. Vivian Hunt, Sara Prince, et al., *Delivering through Diversity*, McKinsey, January 2018, available at www.mckinsey.com/~/media/McKinsey/Business%20Functions/Organization/Our%20Insights/

Delivering%20through%20diversity/Delivering-through-diversity_full-report.ashx

16. Daniel J. Sandberg, 'When women lead, firms win', S&P Global, 16 October 2019, available at www.spglobal.com/en/research-insights/featured/when-women-lead-firms-win

17. Moxie Future, 'Female corporate leaders make firms less likely to fall foul of environmental laws', 27 September 2018, available at moxiefuture.com/2018/09/female-corporate-leaders-make-firms-less-likely-to-fall-foul-of-environmental-laws

18. Sarah Shearman, 'Why "gender-smart" investing is expanding rapidly', World Economic Forum, 22 March 2019, available at www.weforum.org/agenda/2019/03/growth-in-gender-smart-investing-helps-sisters-do-it-for-themselves

19. Najada Kumbuli, Leigh Moran and Jenn Pryce, *Just Good Investing: Why Gender Matters to Your Portfolio and What You Can Do About It*, Calvert Impact Capital, December 2018, available at www.calvertimpactcapital.org/storage/documents/calvert-impact-capital-gender-report.pdf

20. Sarah Shearman, 'Growth in "gender-smart investing" helps sisters do it for themselves', Thomson Reuters Foundation, 8 March 2019, available at news.trust.org//item/20190308105708-ikonv

21. ImpactAlpha, 'Gender-smart investing: more than two dozen new funds investing with a gender lens', available at impactalpha.com/gender-smart-investing-more-than-two-dozen-new-funds-investing-with-a-gender-lens

22. Ibid.

23. Read more at paxworld.com/funds/pax-ellevate-global-womens-leadership-fund

24. Jayna Rana, 'Want to help tackle gender inequality and make a profit? We take a look at LGIM's GIRL fund that's beaten the market since launch', This is Money, 14 September 2019, available at www.thisismoney.co.uk/money/investing/article-7419195/L-Gs-GIRL-fund-wants-tackle-gender-equality-make-profit.html

## ELEVEN: WHO YOU GONNA CALL? – THE ROLE OF THE FINANCIAL ADVISOR

1. WealthiHer, *The WealthiHer Report 2019: Understanding the Diversity of Women's Wealth*, available at www.wealthihernetwork.com/rep

2. Sylvia Ann Hewlett and Andrea Turner Moffitt with Melinda

Marshall, *Harnessing the Power of the Purse: Female Investors and Global Opportunities for Growth*, Center for Talent Innovation, 2014, available at www.talentinnovation.org/_private/assets/HarnessingThePowerOfThePurse_ExecSumm-CTI-CONFIDENTIAL.pdf

3. Eve Kaplan, 'Women have specific financial needs that advisors overlook', *Forbes*, 6 August 2018, available at www.forbes.com/sites/feeonlyplanner/2018/08/06/women-have-specific-financial-needs-that-advisors-overlook/#136c2ec47c04

4. Gary Baker, 'Advisers must adapt to survive', *FT Adviser*, 11 September 2019, available at www.ftadviser.com/your-industry/2019/09/11/advisers-must-adapt-to-survive

5. McKinsey & Company, *The Virtual Financial Advisor: Delivering Personalized Advice in the Digital Age*, 1 June 2015, available at www.mckinsey.com/industries/financial-services/our-insights/the-virtual-financial-advisor-delivering-personalized-advice-in-the-digital-age

6. Mrin Agarwal, 'Viewpoint: How your advisor's personal biases can impact your investments', Money Control, 31 May 2019, available at www.moneycontrol.com/news/business/personal-finance/viewpoint-how-your-advisors-personal-biases-can-impact-your-investments-4050251.html

7. Kristen Bellstrom and Emma Hinchliffe, 'Why more clients want female financial advisers', *Fortune*, 27 August 2019, available at www.fortune.com/2019/08/27/female-financial-advisers

8. Allianz, 'Seniors 65 and older are more interested in ESG strategies than younger generations, finds AllianzGI ESG clarity survey', 17 October 2017, available at us.allianzgi.com/en-us/ria/our-firm/newsroom/press-releases/results-of-2017-esg-survey

9. The Rockefeller Foundation, *The Individual Imperative: Retail Impact Investing Uncovered*, June 2019, available at www.rockefellerfoundation.org/report/individual-imperative-retail-impact-investing-uncovered

10. Karen Demasters, 'Advisors failing to talk ESG with clients', *FA Mag*, 8 November 2017, available at www.fa-mag.com/news/advisors-failing-to-talk-esg-with-clients-35627.html

11. Michael E. Porter, George Serafeim and Mark Kramer, 'Where ESG fails', Institutional Investor, 16 October 2019, available at www.institutionalinvestor.com/article/b1hm5ghqtxj9s7/Where-ESG-Fails

## TWELVE: TECHNOLOGY — A GAME-CHANGER FOR SUSTAINABLE INVESTORS?

1. Stephen Wall, 'Four top uses of technology in wealth management', Raconteur Opinions, 22 July 2019, available at www.raconteur.net/finance/technology-wealth-management

2. Patrick Schueffel, *The Concise Fintech Compendium*, School of Management, Fribourg, Switzerland, 2017, p. 26.

3. Betterment, a US-based robo-advisor, provides some good introductory content on what online financial advice entails. Read more at www.betterment.com/category/robo-advisor

4. Renat Heuberger and Ingo Puhl, '5 ways blockchain can transform the world of impact investing', part of the Sustainable Development Summit, World Economic Forum, 20 September 2018, available at www.weforum.org/agenda/2018/09/5-ways-blockchain-can-transform-the-world-of-impact-investing

5. Huw Van Steenis, 'Defective data is a big problem for sustainable investing', *Financial Times*, 21 January 2019, available at www.ft.com/content/c742edfa-30be-328e-8bd2-a7f8870171e4

6. Read more at www.arabesque.com

7. Sallie Krawcheck, 'Ellevest just raised $34.5 Million. Here's the annotated press release', *Ellevest Magazine*, 28 March 2019, available at www.ellevest.com/magazine/news/ellevest-raised-33-million-annotated-press-release

8. There is increasing evidence that the impacts of climate change, across societies, are affecting women and men differently. Why is this the case? In many countries, women are often responsible for the collection and production of food and water, as well as sourcing of fuel for heating and cooking. Tasks such as these are becoming more difficult for many women. In addition, climate-change-related events such as extreme weather (droughts, floods) have a much greater impact on the poor and most vulnerable – 70 per cent of the world's poor are women. For more details on how climate change is affecting women, you can find out more in the IUCN Gender and Climate Issues Brief: www.iucn.org/resources/issues-briefs/gender-and-climate-change

9. OpenInvest, 'About us', available at www.openinvest.com/about

10. Read more at www.nutmeg.com

11. Jack Apollo George, 'Can tech really democratise investing?', Raconteur, 23 July 2019, available at www.raconteur.net/finance/technology-inclusive-investing

12. For example, read this article by Shannen Wong, 'Why passive investing and sustainability are incompatible', City Wire Asia, 26 September 2018, available at www.citywireasia.com/news/why-passive-investing-and-sustainability-are-incompatible/a1158426

13. Elspeth Goodchild, 'Wealth managers need to adjust their approach to better serve women', AltFi, 8 April 2019, available at www.altfi.com/article/5229_wealth-managers-need-to-adjust-their-approach-to-better-serve-women

14. Financial Alliance for Women, *How Fintechs Can Profit from the Multi-Trillion-Dollar Female Economy*, 2020, available at www.financialallianceforwomen.org/download/how-fintechs-can-profit-from-the-multi-trillion-dollar-female-economy

## THIRTEEN: IT'S OVER TO YOU NOW

1. Read more at www.morganstanley.com/what-we-do/institute-for-sustainable-investing

# ACKNOWLEDGEMENTS

It turns out that acknowledging everybody who has played a part in pulling a book together is a really tough job. I am undoubtedly going to upset someone! So, I am going to start with a blanket thank you – to my sisterhood, you know who you are.

A big shout out to all of the book's supporters – it means the world to me that we hit the funding target so quickly and, more importantly, that you demonstrated your faith in my getting this book written. I would also like to recognise all of those who have been involved in building Moxie Future – our Ambassadors, our Advisory Group and the beautiful Taura Edgar, my wingwoman. And, of course, the team at Unbound – it has been a wonderful experience working with such a positive and supportive publishing team. They have really been amazing – in particular, Fiona Lensvelt and DeAndra Lupu.

So many special individuals have played an important role in my professional and personal development, which, in turn, has got me to the point where I felt comfortable and confident putting pen to paper for *Financial Feminism*. This collective makes up some of the unique and beautiful people who prioritise change for the greater good and know that sustainability and equality must sit at the core of everything we do. Some have given up their free time to review chapters or contribute their thoughts. Some have connected me with people and networks. Some have listened endlessly to my intellectual pontifications. Some have drunk wine with me and dreamed of a brighter future. Some have just simply had my back when I needed it the most.

With too many to name, here are just a few. In no particular order... Anne Copeland, Hannah Routh, Marilyn Robinson, Clare Bolt, Saptarshi Ray, Julian Calder, Dina Storey, Toby Robinson, Sophie Stevens, Cianne Moores, Sherif Shafie, Alex Birkin, Lale Kesebi, Christine Loh, Carey Bohjanen, Glenn Frommer, Alexandra Tracy, Kimberley Cole, Charlotte Wilkinson, Tim Pagett, Sian Rowlands, Mandy Kirby, Hanna Edstrom, Olivia Sibony, Amy Clarke, Ellen Remmer, Karla Mora, Kristin Hull, Suzanne Biegel, Tracy Gray, Patience Marine-Ball, Heather Heynon, Bonny Landers, Julia Dreblow, Kimberley Abbott, Claire Veuthey. Oh, and my FutureWomenX tribe!

A final acknowledgement goes to the many amazing people working in the sustainable investing field – these people are true warriors, forging forward with new ideas and innovative solutions, pushing boundaries and arguing the case to do things better. They have often done this in a world that was not ready and against much resistance. I am truly grateful that I have been part of this global community, and this book really is a reflection of all that we have worked so hard on over the years. Finally, it seems as though the world is starting to listen.

# A NOTE ON THE AUTHOR

Jessica Robinson is the founder of Moxie Future, the world's first education, insights and community platform empowering women as sustainable investors and financial feminists. She also has a day job, working as a strategic advisor to institutional investors, think tanks and governments on all things relating to green finance, sustainability, responsible investment and gender. Having lived and worked all over the world, she is now based in the UAE along with her three children and ever-growing tribe of adopted animals.

# DEDICATIONS

**Women of the World Endowment**
Thank you, WoWE, for your amazing support, and thank you for your vision to do all you can to disrupt the gender landscape! We have so much work to do and WoWE's mission to drive lasting change for women and girls and the communities they empower is at the very heart of it. I am proud that we are on this path together.

www.wowendowment.org

**RS Group and the Sustainable Finance initiative (SFi)**
RS Group and SFi truly lead from the front, inspiring private investors to care about how they deploy their capital and showing that prioritising impact can be done. A wholehearted thank you for your support, in more ways than one – it's been a long journey, but we are finally making progress. Your support for this book is invaluable and I truly hope it will keep the conversation flowing.

www.sustainablefinance.hk

## Hello Sister

Understanding what women want is critical to building the kind of world we want to live in – Hello Sister, thank you for your support, keeping our eyes open to the importance of everyone being heard and partnering with me as we build the female economy. You rock!

www.hellosisterstrategy.com

With an extra special thanks to Lale Kesebi and Timothy Pagett for their truly amazing support for this book.

MOXIE FUTURE

Unbound is the world's first crowdfunding publisher, established in 2011.

We believe that wonderful things can happen when you clear a path for people who share a passion. That's why we've built a platform that brings together readers and authors to crowdfund books they believe in – and give fresh ideas that don't fit the traditional mould the chance they deserve.

This book is in your hands because readers made it possible. Everyone who pledged their support is listed below. Join them by visiting unbound.com and supporting a book today.

Kristina Abbotts
Rachel Alembakis
And from All
Sarah Anderton
Marc Anthonisen
Farzana Aslam
Tatiana Assali
Megan Astbury
Fiona Atkinson
James Bair
Karen Baker
Zena Barrie
Liz Berks

Aditi Bhaskaran
Suzanne Biegel
Vanessa Bingle
Murray Birt
Carey Bohjanen
Clare Bolt
Alice Bordini-Staden
Ellen Boucher
Daniel Bowerman
Jen Braswell
Juliette Brederode
Christine Brendle
Jenny Cameron

Rawya Catto

Kathryn Chabarek

Heidi Chan

Annie Chen

Soo Choi

Lucy Chow

Jeanne Chow Collins

Kimberley Cole

Lyndsey Connolly

Nick Conway

Kevin Conyers

Anne Copeland

Simon Copley

Zoe Cousens

Gemma Cowin

Robert Cox

Kate Craig Waller

Lucy d'Abo

Elizabeth Darracott

Jenny Debley

Lorène Delhoume

Ruth Dobson

S. R. Dreamholde

Taura Edgar

Nefertari Egara

Anne English

Robyn Evans Cunningham

Denisa Fainis

Kshama Fernandes

Carina Ferreira

Laura Foley

Jo Francis

Glenn Frommer

Caroline Gale

Nicola Gammon

Galia Gichon

Jeff Gill

Soazig Goardon

Jau Goh

Mara Gottlieb

Blake Goud

Tracy Gray

Emma Green

Shannon Grewer

Nicola Haggett

Lucy Henzell-Thomas

Cheri Heyse

Sarah Hoblyn

Emily Hodder

James Horsman

Helen Hubert

Tom Hulley

Caroline Hurst

Aileen Irons

Julie Jones

Lizzie Kaye

Helen Keeler

Hilary Kemp

Lale Kesebi

Dan Kieran

Jennifer King

Mandy Kirby

Stephanie Kirchhofer

Laure Korenian-Chabert

Hanisha Kotecha

Marie Kretz Di Meglio

Helene Kreysa
Seth Lachner
Flynn Lebus
Fiona Lensvelt
Anastasia Lewis
Ming Lin
littlepurplegoth
Kirsty Lowe
Alicia Lui
Geilan Malet-Bates
Vanessa Marescialli
Anarella Martinez-Madrid
Richard Mattison
Venetia Maunsell
Rochelle McCune
Mary K. McHale
Zoe McKenzie
Bairbre Meade
Ineke Meijer
Caterina Meloni
John Mitchinson
Kristina Montague
Gabriella Montandon
Cianne Moores
Abebech Moussouamy
Lisa Mulligan
Chitra Nagarajan
Tanja Nagel
Elena Nair
Rebecca Naughten
Carlo Navato
Keilem Ng
Daniela Nicola

Natalie Nietsch
Thos O'Brien
Melanie Osborne
Vanessa Paesani
Tim Pagett
Patience Marime-Ball
Lucie Phipps
Justin Pollard
Edward Potton
Karen Powell
Miriam Price
Phillippa Quinn
Avril Rae
Cat Randle
Samantha Rawlins
Dorian Reece
James Robertson
Ayesha Robinson
Gabrielle Robinson
Helen Robinson
Marilyn Robinson
Thalia Robinson
Toby Robinson
Xiaoli Robinson
Zander Robinson
Sophie Robinson-Tillett
Donna Rossiter
Hannah Routh
Sian Rowlands
Catherine Roy
Astra Rudling
Nick Savage
Carol Sayles

Karen Seymour
Julie Skye
Wendy Staden
Sophie Stevens
Jenni Stewart
Dan Stoddart
Allison Strachan
Anaick Summers
Helena Taylor
Karen Taylor
Asif Teja
Felicity Theaker
Lucy Titley
Julia Trocme-Latter
Christine Tsang
Jenny Tudor
Elissa Turrini
Emmie van Halder

Annelies Van Herwijnen
Claire Veuthey
David Vicary
Elinor Wakefield
Andrew Walsh
Wendy Westbury
Marijn Wiersma
Naomi Wildey
Janice Williams
Sarah Williams
Catherine Williamson
Alana Wilshaw
Dan Chi Wong
Samantha Woods
Ellen Wu
Marilyn Zakhour
Louisa Zeng